Communications
in Computer and Information Science   **1130**

Commenced Publication in 2007
Founding and Former Series Editors:
Phoebe Chen, Alfredo Cuzzocrea, Xiaoyong Du, Orhun Kara, Ting Liu,
Krishna M. Sivalingam, Dominik Ślęzak, Takashi Washio, Xiaokang Yang,
and Junsong Yuan

More information about this series at http://www.springer.com/series/7899

Imen Jemili · Mohamed Mosbah (Eds.)

Distributed Computing for Emerging Smart Networks

First International Workshop, DiCES-N 2019
Hammamet, Tunisia, October 30, 2019
Revised Selected Papers

 Springer

Editors
Imen Jemili (ID)
University of Carthage
Bizerte, Tunisia

Mohamed Mosbah (ID)
Bordeaux INP
Talence, France

ISSN 1865-0929   ISSN 1865-0937 (electronic)
Communications in Computer and Information Science
ISBN 978-3-030-40130-6   ISBN 978-3-030-40131-3 (eBook)
https://doi.org/10.1007/978-3-030-40131-3

This Springer imprint is published by the registered company Springer Nature Switzerland AG
The registered company address is: Gewerbestrasse 11, 6330 Cham, Switzerland

Preface

This volume contains the proceedings of the first Workshop in Distributed Computing for Emerging Smart Networks (DiCES-N 2019). The workshop was held in Hammamet, Tunisia, October 30, 2019, in conjunction with 16th International Colloquium on Theoretical Aspects of Computing (ICTAC 2019). We received a total of 24 submissions, of which 9 were accepted for publication, and an invited talk. The acceptance rate was therefore approximately 37.5%. Reviewing was single-blind, where each paper was assigned to at least three reviewers, and on the average 3.2 Program Committee members.

The workshop tackled issues relative to the design, development, and evaluation of distributed systems, platforms, and architectures for cyber-physical systems in the context of smart cities. The program included three sessions. The first session dealt with "Intelligent Transportation Systems," as one of the principal fields investigated in the context of smart cities. ITS applications aim to offer a seamless transportation experience to roads users, while reducing problems induced by population growth and increased urbanization, such as traffic congestion, air pollution, traffic incidents, etc. The second session was relative to "Distributed Computing for Networking and Communication." In fact, the smart environments can be viewed as interconnection of wide-scale cyber-physical systems, where deployed sensors are gathering diverse information from the surrounding environment and actuators are dynamically changing the environment in some way. To face challenges relative to scalability, energy saving, and resource constraints inherent to these emergent wireless networks, several methods and approaches of distributed computing are exploited in software and hardware to propose new approaches. The third session dealt with "Artificial Intelligence Applied to Cyber-Physical Systems." To manage the huge amount of heterogeneous data gathered from the different sources and environments, the recourse to AI techniques is a per-quisite in order to analyze it and extract valuable knowledge.

We are grateful for the support provided by the many people who contributed to the success of DiCES-N 2019. We received invaluable support from the ICTAC 2019 Steering and Organizing Committees at a number of important times, and particularly from Mr. Slim Kallel. Naturally, the workshop could not have taken place without the efforts made by the Organizing Committee who helped us to organize and publicize the event, particularly the Technical Program Committee (Sabra Mabrouk, Akka Zemmari, and Emna Ben Salem) and the publicity co-chairs (Soumaya Dahi and Rim Negra).

We are also thankful to the members of the Program Committee for providing their valuable time and helping us to review the received papers. We would also like to thank the authors for submitting and then revising a set of high-quality papers. Finally, we express our sincere gratitude to Springer for giving us the opportunity to publish these proceedings, and we appreciate the support and advice provided by Alfred Hofmann, Amin Mobasheri, and Alla Serikova from Springer.

October 2019   Imen Jemili
                                                                   Mohamed Mosbah

Organization

General Co-chairs

Imen Jemili   University of Carthage, Tunisia
Mohamed Mosbah   Bordeaux INP, France

TPC Co-chairs

Sabra Mabrouk   University of Carthage, Tunisia
Emna Ben Salem   University of Carthage, Tunisia
Akka Zemmari   Bordeaux INP, France

Publicity Co-chairs

Soumaya Dahi   University of Carthage, Tunisia
Rim Negra   University of Mannouba, Tunisia

Program Committee

Ihsan Ali   University of Malaya, Malaysia
Raoudha Beltaifa   University of Mannouba, Tunisia
Anis Ben Aicha   University of Carthage, Tunisia
Ahmed El Oualkadi   National School of Applied Sciences of Tangier,
                                 Morocco
Mohammed Erradi   ENSIAS, Morocco
Parvez Faruki   MNIT Jaipur, India
Tahani Gazdar   University of Jeddah, Saudi Arabia
Francine Krief   Bordeaux INP, France
Muhammad Ilyas   University of Malakand, Pakistan
Abderrahmen Mtibaa   Carnegie Mellon University, USA
Rosaura Palma Orozco   National Polytechnic Institute, Mexico
Slim Rekhis   University of Carthage, Tunisia
Ramayah Thurasamy   University of Sains Malaysia, Malaysia
Eiad Yafi   University Kuala Lumpur, Malaysia

Contents

Intelligent Transportation Systems

VANETs Routing Protocols Survey: Classifications, Optimization Methods and New Trends

Chahrazed Ksouri[1,2($\boxtimes$)], Imen Jemili[3], Mohamed Mosbah[1],
and Abdelfettah Belghith[4]

[1] LaBRI, Bordeaux INP, Universiy of Bordeaux, CNRS, Bordeaux, France
chahrazedksouri@gmail.com, mohamed.mosbah@labri.fr
[2] National School of Engineers of Sfax, Sfax, Tunisia
[3] Faculty of Sciences of Bizerte, University of Carthage, Tunis, Tunisia
imen.jmili@fsb.u-carthage.tn
[4] College of Computer and Information Sciences, King Saud University,
Riyadh, Saudi Arabia
abelghith@ksu.edu.sa

Abstract. The specific characteristics of vehicular ad-hoc networks, such as high-speed nodes, frequent topology changes and predefined vehicle movement paths, make mobile ad-hoc networks routing protocols not convenient to disseminate data in the vehicular environment. In addition, the new vision towards Internet of Vehicles concept along with the advent of autonomous cars contribute to the proliferation of new innovative applications with different QoS requirements, rising new challenging issues. In this paper, we survey the different taxonomies for vehicular routing protocols, while exposing several optimization techniques used to enhance routing protocols. Moreover, in order to foster the deployment of robust Internet of Vehicles routing protocols at large scale, we give some directions for future research work.

Keywords: VANETs routing protocols · Classifications · IoV · Optimization techniques · Bio-inspired · Computational intelligence

1 Introduction

Vehicular Ad-hoc Networks (VANETs) remain a hot research topic and tremendous efforts are carried out to deal with their intrinsic issues related to security, mobility, routing, data delivery, etc [1]. These networks offer to vehicular nodes the possibility of exchanging information relative to safety, comfort or entertainment applications [1]. In fact, the architecture of VANETs is composed of vehicles equipped with On Board Units (OBUs) enabling them to communicate with each others and with the Road Side Units (RSUs). In traditional VANETs, we can distinguish between three major communication levels [2]: Vehicle-to-Vehicle communication (V2V), Roadside-to-Vehicle communication (R2V) (also

© Springer Nature Switzerland AG 2020
I. Jemili and M. Mosbah (Eds.): DiCES-N 2019, CCIS 1130, pp. 3–22, 2020.
https://doi.org/10.1007/978-3-030-40131-3_1

referred to as Infrastructure-to-Vehicle communication (I2V)) and hybrid vehicular communication (HVC) (both V2V and R2V). The advent of the Internet of Things paradigm and the recent advancements in communication technologies, have enabled the generalization of VANETs to Internet of Vehicles (IoV) concept. This evolution promoted the emergence of new applications and services with different QoS (Quality of Service) requirements [3]. Furthermore, technological progress associated to autonomous vehicles has reached a mature level and their deployment brings a brand new market of novel advertising services with diverse demands in terms of throughput, latency, jitter, etc. Moreover, such vehicles must be feed continuously with real-time data to maintain their operational status, which increases the need for efficient and robust routing protocols. Vehicles must rely on V2V multi-hop communications to reach remote nodes or whether there is no nearby RSU for direct R2V communications. The routing process is needed in order to relay information between vehicles until reaching the destination. A routing protocol governs the way that entities exchange information; route establishment and packet forwarding are essential component of the routing process, besides required operations for route maintenance and route failure recovery [4]. Despite the enormous work that has been made regarding data delivery in the vehicular context, routing remains a significant challenge. In fact, it still faces the intrinsic characteristics of VANET, such as high speed and frequent topology changes and has to deal with the new imposed exigencies by the various applications and services introduced with the advent of Internet of Vehicles.

A considerable number of surveys has been proposed in the literature, covering different aspects of routing process in the vehicular environment [4–10]. These surveys proposed a specific [4–8] or several [9,10] taxonomies, hence, no one of them gives a holistic view of all existing classifications for VANETs routing protocols. Moreover, in certain works [5,6], they mix categories of different taxonomies, while in others [8], the authors do not explicitly define the criterion used for classification. To the best of our knowledge, this is the first comprehensive work presenting such a survey, which encompasses all possible classifications of routing protocols and presents multitude of optimization techniques and concepts. In addition, we introduce the new challenges brought by IoV to the routing protocol design. Specifically, the key contributions provided by this work are:

- We survey the state-of-the-art routing protocols taxonomies in VANETs and we suggest new criteria for their classification, while providing an exhaustive list of existing terminologies in the literature.
- We present a set of optimization techniques and paradigms that have been introduced, in the past two decades, to improve routing protocols design and management.
- We discuss open research issues and future trends to consider in the Internet of Vehicles routing protocols design.

The remainder of the paper is structured as follows. Section 2 explicitly describes the taxonomies of vehicular routing protocols. In Sect. 3, we present the paradigms that have been used to optimize routing process in the vehicular environment. Then, an insight of the new directives related to routing protocols in Internet of Vehicles is provided in Sect. 4. Finally, we conclude the paper in Sect. 5.

2   Routing Protocols Classifications

VANETs routing protocols may be classified according to several criteria. In this section, we will discuss the different taxonomies, reviewed by previous surveys, and their corresponding nomenclatures. In addition, we introduce new criteria for protocols classification. To conduct this work, we reviewed about 30 surveys proposed between 2006 to 2018. We retained only those with new taxonomies, consistent with other works and with relevant information.

A survey on routing in VANETs was conducted in [5], where the authors used the forwarder selection strategy as criterion to classify routing protocols. Four categories are put forth: position-based, broadcast-based, geocast-based and cluster-based routing protocols. Similarly to this taxonomy [5], a comparative study of various routing protocols in VANETs was carried out in [6], where the authors added a fifth category, topology-based. In [4], a classification according to the routing information used in packet forwarding was presented, the authors distinguish between two categories: topology-based, subdivided into two classes relative to routing strategies namely proactive and reactive, and geographic-based, sub-categorized, depending on the network sensitivity, into delay tolerant and non delay tolerant networks. The authors in [7] proposed another classification according to the transmission mode, namely: unicast, multicast, geoacast and braodcast. In [8], the routing protocols classification is carried out according to the topology, geography, hybrid, clustering, opportunistic and data fusion features.

The authors, in [9], presented a review on Internet of Vehicles routing protocols. The reviewed protocols were classified into five disparate taxonomies, namely: transmission strategy (unicast, geocast and broadcast), required routing information (topology-based, position-based, map-based and path-based), delay sensitivity (delay-sensitive and delay-tolerant), dimension of scenarios (1-D (planar: high-way, street without intersections), 2-D (planar: street with intersections) and 3-D (non-planer: hierarchical structure of road plane)), and target network type (homogeneous and heterogeneous). The classification taxonomy provided in [10] adopted the same categories as in [9]. However, they consider two new perspectives: security sensitivity (insecure strategies and secure strategies) and network architecture (traditional and SDN-based architectures).

2.1   Existing Taxonomies

In this sub-section, we will detail and discuss the different taxonomies addressed by previous surveys:

Forwarder Selection: Forwarder selection was the first criterion to be used to classify vehicular routing protocols, as this step can affect deeply the performance of the routing process. It was presented initially in [5] and adopted by almost all classification surveys conducted afterword [4, 6, 8–10]. According to this criterion, we distinguish mainly between:

- **Topology-based** approaches, which select forwarding nodes based on the network topology information [7]. Before transmitting a data packet, a route is established through control packets. To cope with the highly dynamic changes of the vehicular topology, this approach may overhead the network with control packets which makes it not suitable for VANETs networks, especially in dense scenarios.
- **Geography-based** routing, where several geographical metrics were stated to perform forwarding namely: location, position, mobility (speed, direction, velocity). Such information can be retrieved from street maps (map-based protocols [9]), navigational systems such as global positioning system [11], the vehicle sensors and location services.

Dissemination Strategy: To meet the application requirements, several transmission strategies may be used in the vehicular environment. A routing protocol can handle one or more dissemination strategies. This classification, presented in [7, 12], distinguishes between:

- **Unicast:** The main goal of a unicast routing in VANETs is to transmit data from a single source to a single destination via wireless multi-hop transmissions or store-carry-forward techniques (SCF) [12], where the node carries the packet until it reaches the destination or a relaying node.
- **Multicast:** A multicast transmission allows to send packets from a single source to specific group members by multi-hop communication or SCF [12].
- **Broadcast:** The primary objective of broad-casting in VANETs is to disseminate information from a source to many unspecified destinations [7].
- **Geocast** routing, also described as a location-based multi-cast routing [5], is a special case where nodes in a certain geographic location (Zone of Relevance, ZOR or Zone of Interest, ZOI) can be the destinations [5], also called GeoBroadcast [13]. If the destination is one node located in a certain position, we call it GeoUnicast [13].

Beacon: Beacons are packets exchanged periodically among nodes to inform about position, speed, direction, etc. Such useful information may be exploited by routing process, MAC protocols and many applications such ADAS (Advanced Driver-Assistance Systems) applications. We can distinguish between two categories [4]: **Beacon-based** protocols using information gathered from beacons to perform route discovery, forwarding, maintenance and recovery, and **Beacon-less** protocols that do not rely on such information. To reduce the network overhead related to beacon-based approaches, many adaptive beaconing mechanisms have been proposed in the literature [14].

Delay Sensitivity: The delay sensitivity criterion was introduced in [4] and reconsidered in [9,10]; it is tightly related to the traffic type. In fact, safety-related applications are **non tolerant delay (time-sensitive)** since the data must be disseminated in a timely manner to keep the information relevance. In contrast, comfort and some infotainment applications, called **delay-tolerant (time-insensitive)** applications, can tolerate disruptive and intermittent network connectivity. A routing protocol can be designed to manage only one or both types of traffic.

Routing Strategy: The routing strategy classification was primarily proposed by authors in [4] and completed by [15]. We can distinguish between three routing strategies in the vehicular context [15]:

- **Proactive** protocols: Also known as **table driven** routing protocols [15], they keep an updated routing table thanks to the periodic exchange of control packets between neighbours to maintain the links states [4]. This protocols family achieves low latency since routing information (path towards the destination) is available upon lookup. However, it consumes a great part of the network bandwidth, especially in high density networks.
- **Reactive** routing protocols, also called **on-demand**, establish a route when it is requested by a node to send packets [4]. In contrast with proactive routing, this category of protocols does not consume a lot of bandwidth. However, the discovery process initiated to establish the path towards the destination leads to a high latency.
- **Hybrid** routing combines attractive features of both proactive and reactive mechanisms in order to minimize the control overhead and reduce the delay of the route discovery process relative to on-demand routing protocols [15].

Target Network: The network technology recently became a criterion upon which routing protocols can be classified [9], as many communication technologies can be used to exchange information between the vehicular components (vehicles, RSUs, road signs, etc), to cite a few examples: DSRC (Dedicated Short Range Communication), 5G, LiFi (Light Fidelity) [16]. For V2V communications, the main deployed technologies are DSRC and cellular communications [17]. Based on the target networks, we can distinguish between two network models [9]: **homogeneous** network, where one technology is used and **heterogeneous** network, where two or more technologies are deployed. Routing protocols can be designed to operate in one of these two environments [17].

Network Dimensions: As stated in [9], the classification of routing protocols according to the network dimension can be divided into three categories:

- The one dimension,**1-D**, category, also referred to as planar, encompasses highway and street without intersections, where vehicles are spread over one or more lanes and move at the same direction or the exact opposite one.
- The two dimensions, **2-D**, is also planar and encompasses street with intersections, where more than two routing directions are possible.

– Three dimensional networks, **3-D**, are non-planer and they have a hierarchical structure of road plane with a vertical direction for routing [18].

Security Sensitivity: This classification was recently proposed by [10]. In fact, the real deployment of connected and autonomous cars and the emergence of new cyber attacks underscore the need to step up efforts to secure vehicle routing protocols. Two categories of routing protocols can be recognized from this perspective [10]: **secure strategies**, integrating security mechanisms and **insecure strategies**.

2.2 Discussion

Taxonomy based on forwarder selection is one of the most used VANETs routing protocol classifications [4–6,8–10]. However, each one of these works proposed a different taxonomy. Inspired by existing works in the literature, we suggest a new taxonomy based on forwarder selection criterion, where we maintain only the macro classification proposed by [4] (topology-based and geographic-based), as it was shown by [8–10] that not only geographic-based routing protocols can be sub-categorized depending on the network sensitivity, neither only topology-based protocols can be subdivided according to the routing strategy. In addition we sub-classify the geographic-based into position-based and mobility-based protocols, since they both use geographic information. Geographic routing is more suitable for the vehicular environment, as it scales efficiently in large networks since it only uses geographical information of nearby nodes to select the next forwarder instead of the complete network graph that topology protocols require [19]. Indeed, it was adopted by ETSI (European Telecommunications Standards Institute) as the basis of the official routing protocol, GeoNetworking [13], for Intelligent Transportation Systems. Based on geographical metrics, we can distinguish between two categories:

– **Position/Location/Distance-based** routing protocols use location information in order to take routing decisions. Every node is supposed to know its position, the positions of its neighbours and the coordinates of the destination [7]. This category of routing does not need routing discovery and maintenance phases, which lighten network overload.
– **Mobility-based** routing protocols, also referred to as **path-based** [9], consider mobility related information such as speed and velocity, while making routing decisions, in order to cope with the high mobility conditions of VANETs [11]. **Trajectory/Direction-based** forwarding scheme is a specific case of this class, where the data packet is transmitted along a trajectory pre-computed by the source [20]. The information relative to the forwarding direction is included in the header of the message. The node in front of the current packet holder and closest to the specified path is selected as the relay node [20]. The possibility of reaching a point where no neighbour node exists to relay the packet represents the main drawback of this solution.

Besides, many criteria can be used to offer other classifications. However, they were not reported by the previous surveys as taxonomy bases for vehicular routing protocols. We cite among them:

Environment: The targeted environment influences the protocols design. In the context of VANETs, properties such as speed limits and safe following distances differ from one mobility model to another, specific to each zone or location. The environment criterion was adopted by other surveys [12, 15, 21] in summarising tables. They are three, namely:

- The **Urban** environment, corresponding to a city center, is characterized by an ubiquitous infrastructure providing direct R2V communications.
- **Highways** connect cities together. The vehicle's speed is higher than in urban areas and the movement paths are more predefined, as there is less exits.
- **Rural** areas are situated at the suburbs of cities, and are, mostly, characterized by a low traffic compared to the others environments. In addition, the infrastructure is nearly non-existent and vehicles must rely exclusively on V2V communications.

Application: The routing protocols can be designed to handle one or multiple types of traffic, as each application may have its own QoS needs. This classification results from the diversification of VANETs applications and services [22], we distinguish between:

- **Safety information** need to be delivered in a timely manner. Thus, the most important aspect of safety-related routing protocols is the delay metric.
- **Infotainment/Advertising** applications require a communication with a high Qos so the corresponding routing protocols have to satisfy criterion like end-to-end delay and QoE (Quality of Experience).
- **Comfort** applications are more delay tolerant that the other ones.

Objective: We can differentiate between two categories of vehicular routing protocols: **mono-objective protocols** and **multi-objective protocols** [23]. The routing process tries to find the best route with one or multiple criteria such as end-to-end delay, QoE, hop number, transmission cost, the stability of the links, congestion, dense or sparse network, etc. The choice of the criteria is tightly related to the traffic type of the applications.

Layer Information: For routing process, the protocol can rely on a **single-layer** or a **cross-layer** design [11]. Cross-layer design exploits the dependency between protocol layers to achieve the better performances. In fact, it allows information exchange between physical, medium access control and network layers to optimise routing process. Such techniques were surveyed in [11]. Table 1 presents the different routing parameters associated to each layer, based on [11]. Besides, we added the neighbours number as a network metric used for the forwarder selection.

Table 1. Layers routing parameters

Layer	Routing parameters
Physical	• RSSI: Received Signal Strength Indicator • SINR: Signal-to-Interference-plus-Noise Ratio • SNR: Signal-to-Noise Ratio • Packet error rate: is based on the bit error rate, calculated using SINR information • Channel rate: the tight upper bound on the rate at which information can be reliably transmitted over a communication channel
Mac	• Mac frame error rate: is based on the packet error rate • Queuing information: gives information regarding buffer space • Retransmission count: is recorded along the path from source to destination • Inter-arrival time: is the time elapsed between two consecutive packet arrivals in the queue • Packet train size: reflects the average value of the number of packets sent in a single transmission period • Service time: is the total time required for channel contention and actual transmission
Network	• Hop count: the number of hops between source and destination • Neighbours number: number of nodes in the coverage area

Communication System: The vehicular ecosystem encompasses mobile nodes (vehicles) and fixed ones (infrastructure) and several communications systems ensure the data exchange between these elements namely; Vehicle-to-Vehicle communication (V2V), Roadside-to-Vehicle communication (R2V) and both (hybrid) [2]. A vehicular node communicates directly with another one forming a one hop communication, otherwise if there is no direct connection, then vehicles execute a routing protocol to forward messages from one node to another until reaching the destination (vehicle or infrastructure). According to the communication system criterion, we can distinguish between routing protocols that do use only V2V communications and those that do rely on both V2V and V2I communications to deliver the packet to the destination. In the second case, to reach their destination, vehicles may rely on information sent by the infrastructure to route the packet, or they may transmit the data to the infrastructure that will take care of sending the packet to the destination. The integration of VANETs with new concepts such as Cloud Computing and Software Defined Networking, detailed in the following sections, encouraged such hybrid solution.

3 Routing Protocols Optimization Techniques and Paradigms

Different optimization techniques are used to improve several aspects of routing; decision making, path discovery, relay node selection, routing failure recovery, cluster head selection, etc. Through this section, we present classical concepts used for vehicular routing, while pointing out recently proposed ones. For both, we refer to the introducing publication and present only the recent works that use them. Among these techniques we cite:

3.1 Bio-inspired

The bio-inspired techniques, also know as heuristic-based methods, look at biology as a source of inspiration and reproduce the laws and dynamics of natural species in the computational world [23–25]. The use of bio-inspired approaches in the designing of routing protocols has been widely used, as communication scenarios in networking are so similar to the natural communication of species. Basic principles relative to local cooperation between neighbours and local communication to attain global information about the state of the network allow to address VANETs routing limitations, such as lack of scalability, self-organization control and routing complexity. In [23], the authors classified the bio-inspired schemes into three main categories:

- **Evolutionary Algorithms:** This category consists of computational techniques inspired by natural evolution and genetic such as selection, crossover, mutation [23] [25]. These approaches aim to find the best solution for hard optimization problems such as finding the optimal route between the source and the destination in VANETs routing case. Both works proposed in [26] and [27] addressed broadcast storm problem thought controlling retransmissions by using, respectively, an analytical fitness function and an optimized relay selection methodology based on multi-objective genetic algorithm.
- **Swarm Intelligence:** This class groups all VANETs routing algorithms inspired by swarm intelligence such as ants, firefly, bees, birds, etc. Swarm Intelligence, or distributed intelligence, is a concept based on the coordination between a massive number of individual actions [28]. It is the collective behaviour resulting from local interactions between several individuals to fulfill global complex tasks (food searching, reproduction, defense, etc.) [23]. Ants Colony Optimization (ACO), one of the most studied swarm optimization techniques, is based on the imitation of their use of pheromone trails in order to indirectly communicate with each other and inform about the route to the food source [29]. In [30], authors proposed an ACO-based traffic-aware VANETs protocol for city environments in order to find the optimal routing path. A weight function is calculated for each road segment on the network. The one with the minimum weight is designated as the best route. Authors, in [31], presented a novel selective cross layer based routing scheme using ACO method for vehicular networks, where ACO is used to resolve the route

selection issue. Particle Swarm Optimization (PSO) algorithms, another bio-inspired approach, are designed in a way enabling particles, defined by their positions and velocities, to choose among the best previously encountered positions or move towards a new better one. This approach takes its roots from fish schooling and bird flocking [32]. A PSO-based optimized multi-path routing for VANETs was proposed in [33]. The list of optimal paths available is determined by employing PSO-based method. Then, a learning automata is used to evaluate if the candidate paths can be used for transmission. Finally, the path breaks are predetermined using Leapfrog algorithm. In [34], the authors proposed a routing protocol for VANETs, exploiting the PSO technique as backbone of angular routing to determine a suitable routing path to carry a message from source to destination. As another swarm intelligence representation, Bees Colony Optimization (BCO) algorithm is inspired by the food foraging behaviour of honey bees. After the harvesting season, where scout bees were foraging, once returned to the hive, they inform other bees about the direction towards flowers, its distance from the hive and its quality rating (or fitness), by performing the dance floor [35]. To improve reliability of roadside-to-vehicle communication in VANETs, the work, in [36], proposed a binary coded artificial bee colony algorithm to obtain several alternatives to a minimum spanning tree. A QoS-aware routing in vehicular ad hoc networks using bee colony optimization was proposed in [37]. We, also, find in the literature routing protocols optimization inspired from feline species such as cat [38]. Cat Swarm Optimization (CSO) allows imitating the two major behaviours of cats, seeking and tracking. In [39], the authors proposed a geographic routing algorithm based on CSO in order to find optimal position of next forwarding node efficiently based on a fitness function.

– **Other Bio-inspired Approaches:** According to [23], other bio-inspired approaches can be grouped into two categories: natural immune systems and algorithms inspired by human social behaviour. Typical example for the first category is the imitation of harvesting behaviour of certain bacteria when searching nutrient [40]. Authors, in [41], were the only ones to exploit Bacterial Foraging Optimization (BFO) algorithm for finding route in VANETs. The BFO was used to find the shortest route in a limited period, as it ensure scalibility. The second category encompasses algorithms inspired by human social behaviours (emotions, hypnosis, coercion), where socially-inspired foraging and deference strategies were proposed, such as the work in [42]. The authors presented three channel selection strategies; where two are bio-socially inspired and are framed as evolutionary game based on prevalent behaviours in human societies such as resource sharing. The first one considers that each user competes simultaneously with all other users over all channels. The second one assumes that the system is evolving if users change strategies over time in order to adopt more efficient one, used by their neighbours. Nature based optimization algorithms were not presented in previous works, such as the Water Wave Optimization (WWO) proposed in [43]. The WWO technique takes its roots from the water wave theory [44], it combines three operators related to water wave namely propagation, refraction and breaking to establish a good balance between exploration and exploitation. In fact, as detailed in [43], the propagation operator searches small areas employing high fitness waves and explores large areas using low fitness ones; the refraction operator helps to resolve issues related to search stagnation, thus improving the diversity of the population and reducing premature convergence; the breaking operator enables an intensive search around a (potentially) promising area. This technique was adopted for VANETs in [45] to find the optimal route based on a multi-constrained QoS measures. Also not reviewed by anterior works, algorithms that mimic the social behaviour of marine species such as whales are found in the literature [46]. Whale Optimization Algorithm (WOA) is inspired by the bubble-net hunting strategy of humpback whales, which consists of creating distinctive bubbles in a spiral shape around the prey and swim up toward the surface. Authors, in [47], proposed an enhanced whale optimization algorithm for vehicular communication networks. The WOA is used for cluster organizing and cluster head election in order to enhance the mobility management by evaluating the trust value in the traffic system.

3.2   Computational Intelligence

The computational intelligence field, recently popularized as Artificial Intelligence (AI), has experimented an amazing growth in the last years and new branches of the discipline are emerging continuously. Several techniques were adopted to enhance routing algorithms in the vehicular environment, among these we quote:

- **Fuzzy logic** (FL) or probabilistic logic, is a soft computing tool relying on approximate modes of reasoning rather than exact ones [48]. In fact, FL uses a set of variables with a truth value ranging in degree between 0 and 1, in contrast to binary logic where variables may take only 0 or 1 values [23]. In VANETs routing, these techniques are used to improve the decision-making and reduce delays in computation [49,50]. In [49], authors proposed a routing protocol based on fussy logic systems in order to deal with coordination and analysis of contradicting metrics, such as vehicles' position, direction, link quality and achievable throughput. The aim is to select the most suitable next-hop for packet forwarding. Authors, in [50], proposed a compressed fuzzy logic based multi-criteria AODV routing in VANETs environment. This proposition aims to enhance the routing decision mechanism by jointly considering number of relays, distance factor, direction angle and vehicles speed variance.
- **Reinforcement Learning** (RL) is the most used branch of machine learning [51] for solving vehicular routing problems. RL is a technique used to build autonomous systems improving themselves with experience [52]. In fact, it provides a framework by which a system can learn from its previous interactions with its environment to automatically raise the efficacy of its own execution [52]. RL is mainly used to solve optimization problems relative to distributed systems such as routing process [53]. A RL based Hybrid Routing

algorithm (RHR) that tracks the simultaneously available paths to a specific destination was presented in [54]. A Reinforcement learning mechanism is run for each route in the forwarding table to guide routing. Authors, in [55], presented an adaptive routing protocol based on reinforcement learning in order to learn and obtain the up-to-date network link status by using distributed Q-learning algorithm. The same algorithm was used in [56] to evaluate the quality of links of the neighbour nodes in order to select the next-hop, while maintaining the stability and reliability of routing.

– **Game theory** (GT) is a branch of applied mathematics, used to study interactions among rational participants in a multiagent decision making process [57]. GT makes the participants able to observe the behaviours of each other in the past and adjust accordingly their strategies [57]. Several based-Game theory relay selection schemes were proposed for VANETs routing protocols. In order to avoid frequent cluster reformation due to the rapid changes in the network topology, authors in [58] proposed a evolutionary GT framework to automate the cluster formation and the cluster head nomination. The framework enables to achieve cluster stability in VANETs. Authors, in [59], proposed a GT approach for multimedia transmission in platoon-based driving. The idea of the proposed GT scheme is to encourage platoon members to cooperate in order to ensure video dissemination services, by offering reward (e.g., money or coupon).

3.3   Software Defined Networking

Software Defined Networking (SDN) is a networking paradigm that decouples the control plane from the data plane and enables the communication between them through an Application Programming Interface (API) [60, 61]. The concept was introduced, at first, to surmount the shortcomings of traditional networks, expensive to update and dedicated to only one service at a time [10]. One of the major outcomes of the paradigm is the design of programmable and flexible networking architecture [62]. In an SDN architecture, the controller, a logically centralized entity situated at the control plane, is responsible for monitoring and managing the network resources, whereas the data plane encompasses the networking infrastructure made of forwarding devices and wired/wireless communication links [62]. Several SDN based Vehicular Ad-hoc Network (SDNV) architectures were proposed to improve the performances of VANETs, while tackling different aspects: routing, security, management, etc [62]. In fact, the use of SDN allows the network to respond better to sudden topology changes and to handle scalability issues, inherent to vehicular environment. In SDNV, routing decisions are taken at the controller level and communicated to the vehicles. Thus, more efficient routing decisions will be made thanks to the global view of the controller upon the network. In addition, the network overhead will be alleviated since vehicles will not have to exchange control messages to establish routes or to handle path failures, therefore reducing processing time and achieving lower end-to-end delay. We can distinguish between **centralized, distributed** and **hybrid** SDNV architectures. In the first category, a centralized controller is responsible for managing the whole network. For instance, in [63], the authors presented a geocast protocol for SDNV in urban areas, where each routing client vehicle transmits periodically state messages (current location and speed) to the routing server that updates the network state. If the packet destination exists in the client routing table, it will be delivered directly. Otherwise, a request message is sent to the routing server that computes the optimal routing paths based on the gathered information. Authors, in [64], presented the Optimal Resource Utilization Routing (ORUR), a new routing scheme incorporating load balancing and congestion prevention. Based on ORUR, the SDN controller takes into account other existing and active routing paths in the VANET to route data on road segments. However, according to [65], performances of centralized SDN-based VANETs drop in large scale. In addition, the SDN controller may fail, consequently degrading the network throughput. For these reasons, the distributed SDNV architecture was proposed, where the control plane is totally distributed. In this context, authors, in [65], proposed a decentralized SDNV architecture which addresses the scalability issue of the vehicular environment. The control plane is partitioned into multiple controllers that are physically distributed across the network and each has a specific knowledge of its region. To keep the consistent knowledge of a centralized controller while guaranteeing the scalability handling feature of a distributed approach, a hybrid version was proposed, where the control of only some details may be delegated to local agents instead of being handled by the controllers. In [66], the authors proposed a V2V-based distributed software-defined networking architecture for infrastructure-less vehicular networks. The decentralized solution proposes to combine SDN with clustering technique to partition the network and assign for each partition a dedicated controller. The mobile SDN controllers cooperate to get a global view of the network state, thus forming a logically centralized but physically distributed multihop control plane.

3.4   Cloud Computing and Fog Computing

Some vehicular applications and services need high computational capabilities to be performed. In this context, using **Cloud Computing** functionalities seems to be an attractive alternative to enable such greedy applications, as it provides, via Internet, a set of plentiful resources, such as powerful computational tools and storage resources [67]. Integrating Cloud Computing to VANETs allows supporting aspects such as security, privacy, scalability and routing [68]. The routing protocol, proposed in [69] for a city environment, exploits Cloud Computing capabilities. In this protocol, vehicle information is sent to the cloud storage through the RSU, thus the information of all the vehicles moving in the city is maintained by the cloud. To reach their destinations, the vehicles send the data to the nearby RSU, which will send a request to the cloud for the optimal RSU information. Cloud will provide location service and then the RSU will send the data to the designated RSU, which will deliver the data to the final destination. Cloud Computing integrating VANETs tackled from another major theme of research which is Vehicular Cloud Computing (VCC). As initially presented in [70], the concept consists of instantly realizing an autonomous cloud among vehicles in order to share their on-board computational, storage and sensing capabilities. To provide free services without any additional infrastructure, authors in [71] proposed a Cooperation as a Service (CaaS) in VANETs. CaaS services were used to perform routing by structuring the network into clusters. For intra-cluster communications, Content Based Routing (CBR) was used, while a geographic routing is adopted for inter-cluster communications. Nevertheless, new exigences in term of real-time processing and QoS were added with the advent of autonomous and connected cars and the exchange of multimedia data relative to IoV applications. To mitigate the lack of real-time processing and to guarantee a minimum QoS threshold, **Fog Computing** was introduced, bringing Cloud Computing capabilities closer to users in order to achieve high bandwidth, low latency and high reliability, especially for remote critical applications [72]. In [73], the authors proposed a fog-based real-time vehicular network mechanism, where RSUs behave as a fog entities to monitor the traffic. This approach aims to relieve the traffic congestion by assisting in managing the flow of vehicles in cities. Similar to Cloud Computing, relaying on a temporarily autonomous fog among vehicles was proposed in [74]. Vehicular Fog Computing (VFC) depends on the collaboration of near-located vehicles resources, thus reducing the deployment costs and time-delay [74]. In fact, in VCC, the vehicles are considered as under-utilized computational resource; integrating the cloud as nodes permit to rent out their in-vehicle capabilities on demand through Internet [70]. A Fog Computing enabling geographic routing in urban areas was proposed in [75] in order to make the best utilization of the vehicular communication and computational resources. Based on the street map and the position of vehicles, it selects the routing path according to the packet error rate of each link and vehicle density of each street.

3.5   Discussion

For more robust and efficient routing protocols and to speed up convergence, some works proposed to combine two or more of the aforementioned optimization techniques. Each one of the aforementioned optimization techniques tackles one aspect of routing process, combining many of them allows to deal with several issues at once. For example, a computational intelligence inspired data delivery for Vehicle-to-Roadside communications combining GT, FL and RL was proposed in [76]. The main goal of the introduced work is to present a totally distributed clustering approach that does not require explicit cluster join/leave messages. A GT approach is used to stimulate the vehicles to join a cluster in order to reduce the number of sender nodes in the network, thus improving the channel contention efficiency at the MAC layer. Then, a FL algorithm is employed to generate stable clusters by considering multiple metrics of vehicle: velocity, mobility pattern and signal qualities in the cluster head selection phase. Finally, to guide each vehicle to select the route that can maximize the whole network performance, a RL algorithm with game theory based reward allocation is employed. Some works proposed the integration of computational intelligence and bio-inspired techniques, such as in [41], where the authors presented a fuzzy bacterial foraging optimization based routing protocol exploiting both BFO and FL techniques. While BFO algorithm was used to find the best route in limited period, FL was implemented to handle uncertain conditions of VANETs. In [77], a fuzzy bio-inspired fog-based distributed routing was presented, where waiting vehicles at urban intersections dynamically form a vehicular fog and proactively establish multihop links with adjacent intersections, in order to analyze the traffic conditions on adjacent road segments using fuzzy logic. The ACO technique was employed to identify an optimal routing path based on the fuzzy logic scheme results. A delay minimization routing algorithm for SDNVs using machine learning to predicts vehicles mobility patterns was introduced in [78]. To perform mobility predictions based on the gathered data from RSUs and compute optimal routing paths, the SDN controller is assisted by an advanced artificial neural network technique.

4 Open Research Issues and Future Trends

The emergence of new technologies such as connected cars has led to the evolution of VANETs towards a more general concept, Internet of Vehicles. IoV plays a prominent role in the Intelligent Transportation Systems for Smart Cities. In fact, it enlarges the vision of Smart Mobility through the introduction of a panoply of communication levels namely: Vehicle-to-Pedestrian, Vehicle-to-Sensor, Vehicle-to-Device, Vehicles-to-Infrastructure, Vehicle-to-Grid [3]. Therefore, by enabling communication among all the ecosystem components, Smart Cities will be able to transport people and goods more safely, efficiently and environmentally.

In a previous work, we identify three network categories including terrestrial, aerial and marine [16]. In fact, the term vehicle includes all transportation means. In the aerial domain, the proliferation of new services, such as drone delivery, taxi drone and medical drone will lead, in the near future, to an overcrowding, especially in Urban Aerial Mobility (UAM) domain. Likewise, in the marine domain, services such autonomous cargo ship and unmanned surface vehicle are in rising popularity. In [9,10], the authors reported routing in Internet of Vehicles, while considering only VANETs as small scale and homogeneous IoV [9] and excluding the aerial and marine domains. Furthermore, some proposed solutions, in the literature, emphasis the interaction among terrestrial and aerial vehicles, such as on-demand routing for urban VANETs using cooperating Unmanned Aerial Vehicles (UAVs) [79], also known as Flying VANETS (FVANETs).

Future routing protocols for Internet of Vehicles must take into account:

- Adaptive and cross-layer approaches are needed to take into account the dynamics of the network and the environment constraints and to meet the application specificities and needs in term of QoS, QoE, end-to-end delay, etc.
- Support the cooperation of vehicles from the different IoV domains (terrestrial, aerial and marine) by enabling them to exchange information.

- With the cohabitation of different communication technologies for data exchange in the vehicular context, routing protocols must be designed to work in a hybrid environment.
- In the era of connected and autonomous vehicles, security of communications and privacy must be on the podium of concerns when designing routing protocols.

5 Conclusion

In this paper, we provide a survey on routing protocols in VANETs context. Routing, in such dynamic environment, remains a widely open research topic, especially with the proliferation of new IoV applications and the emergence of autonomous vehicles, bringing new QoS and security challenges. First, we present the different taxonomies and their variants to allow new researchers to position their work. Second, we highlight some optimization techniques used to come up with more efficient and robust routing algorithms. Finally, we discuss some of the most significant future research directions for the development of large-scale IoV routing protocols. As a continuity to this work, we would like to specify the different techniques used in route discovery, forwarder selection, maintenance and failure recovery phases, and to thoroughly, discuss the recent corresponding works. The vision of Smart Mobility requires a deep cooperation between all modes of transport, and in its role as a catalyst for communications, routing will play a prominent role in the achievement of this integration. As future work, we would like to conduct a similar study in the aerial and marine domains in order to provide a holistic view of IoV routing protocols.

Acknowledgment. This work was financially supported by the "PHC Utique" program of the French Ministry of Foreign Affairs and Ministry of higher education and research and the Tunisian Ministry of higher education and scientific research in the CMCU project number 17G1417.

References

1. Yousefi, S., Mousavi, M.S., Fathy, M.: Vehicular ad hoc networks (VANETs): challenges and perspectives. In: 2006 6th International Conference on ITS Telecommunications, pp. 761–766, June 2006
2. Sichitiu, M.L., Kihl, M.: Inter-vehicle communication systems: a survey. IEEE Commun. Surv. Tutor. **10**(2), 88–105 (2008)
3. Ang, L.M., Seng, K.P., Ijemaru, G.K., Zungeru, A.M.: Deployment of IoV for smart cities: applications, architecture, and challenges. IEEE Access **7**, 6473–6492 (2019)
4. Lee, K.C., Lee, U., Gerla, M.: Survey of routing protocols in vehicular ad hoc networks (2010)
5. Li, F., Wang, Y.: Routing in vehicular ad hoc networks: a survey. IEEE Veh. Technol. Mag. **2**(2), 12–22 (2007)
6. Kumar, R., Dave, M.: A comparative study of various routing protocols in VANET. Int. J. Comput. Sci. Issues **8**, 08 (2011)

7. Chen, W., Guha, R.K., Kwon, T.J., Lee, J., Hsu, I.Y.: A survey and challenges in routing and data dissemination in vehicular ad-hoc networks, pp. 328–333, September 2008

8. Dua, A., Kumar, N., Bawa, S.: A systematic review on routing protocols for vehicular ad hoc networks. Veh. Commun. 1(1), 33–52 (2014)

9. Cheng, J., Cheng, J., Zhou, M., Liu, F., Gao, S., Liu, C.: Routing in Internet of Vehicles: a review. IEEE Trans. Intell. Transp. Syst. 16(5), 2339–2352 (2015)

10. Alouache, L., Nguyen, N., Aliouat, M., Chelouah, R.: Survey on IoV routing protocols: security and network architecture. Int. J. Commun. Syst. 32, e3849 (2019)

11. Awang, A., Husain, K., Kamel, N., Aïssa, S.: Routing in vehicular ad-hoc networks: a survey on single- and cross-layer design techniques, and perspectives. IEEE Access 5, 9497–9517 (2017)

12. Lin, Y.-W., Chen, Y.-S., Lee, S.-L.: Routing protocols in vehicular ad hoc networks: a survey and future perspectives. J. Inf. Sci. Eng. 26, 05 (2010)

13. ETSI: Intelligent transport systems (ITS), vehicular communications; geonetworking, part 1: Requirements. EN 302 636–1 V1.2.1, April 2014

14. Shah, S.A.A., Ahmed, E., Xia, F., Karim, A., Shiraz, M., Noor, R.M.: Adaptive beaconing approaches for vehicular ad hoc networks: a survey. IEEE Syst. J. 12(2), 1263–1277 (2018)

15. Jagadeesh, K., Laxmi, G., Sathya, S., Battula, B.: A survey on routing protocols and its issues in VANET. Int. J. Comput. Appl. 28, 38–44 (2011)

16. Ksouri, C., Jemili, I., Mosbah, M., Belghith, A.: Data gathering for Internet of Vehicles safety. In: 2018 14th International Wireless Communications Mobile Computing Conference (IWCMC), pp. 904–909, June 2018

17. Zekri, A., Jia, W.: Heterogeneous vehicular communications: a comprehensive study. Ad Hoc Netw. 75, 52–79 (2018)

18. Brummer, A., German, R., Djanatliev, A.: On the necessity of three-dimensional considerations in vehicular network simulation. In: 2018 14th Annual Conference on Wireless On-demand Network Systems and Services (WONS), February 2018

19. Katsaros, K.: A survey of routing protocols for vehicular ad-hoc networks (VANETs) (2011)

20. Kayhan, G., Marwan, M., Jaime, L., Rulnizam, K., Bakar, A., Zaitul, Z.: Routing protocols in vehicular ad hoc networks: survey and research challenges. Netw. Protoc. Algorithms 5, 39 (2013)

21. Da Cunha, F.D., Boukerche, A., Villas, L., Viana, A.C., Loureiro, A.A.: Data communication in VANETs: a survey, challenges and applications. Ad Hoc Netw. 44, 90–103 (2016)

22. Willke, T.L., Tientrakool, P., Maxemchuk, N.F.: A survey of inter-vehicle communication protocols and their applications. IEEE Commun. Surv. Tutor. 11(2), 3–20 (2009)

23. Mellouk, A., Bitam, S., Zeadally, S.: Bio-inspired routing algorithms survey for vehicular ad hoc networks. IEEE Commun. Surv. Tutor. 17, 843–867 (2014)

24. Dressler, F., Akan, O.B.: A survey on bio-inspired networking. Comput. Netw. 54(6), 881–900 (2010)

25. Hajlaoui, R., Guyennet, H., Moulahi, T.: A survey on heuristic-based routing methods in vehicular ad-hoc network: technical challenges and future trends. IEEE Sens. J. 16(17), 6782–6792 (2016)

26. Jafer, M., Khan, M.A., ur Rehman, S., Zia, T.A.: Broadcasting under highway environment in VANETs using genetic algorithm. In: 2017 IEEE 85th Vehicular Technology Conference (VTC Spring), pp. 1–5, June 2017

27. Jafer, M., Khan, M.A., Ur Rehman, S., Zia, T.A.: Evolutionary algorithm based optimized relay vehicle selection in vehicular communication. IEEE Access **6**, 71524–71539 (2018)
28. https://www.lebigdata.fr/swarm-intelligence-distribuee-definition
29. Marco, D., Vittorio, M., Alberto, C.: Ant system: optimization by a colony of cooperating agents. IEEE Trans. Syst., Man Cybern. **26**, 29–41 (1996)
30. Goudarzi, F., Asgari, H., Al-Raweshidy, H.S.: Traffic-aware VANET routing for city environments–a protocol based on ant colony optimization. IEEE Syst. J. **13**(1), 571–581 (2019)
31. Gawas, M.A., Gawas, M.M.: A novel selective cross layer based routing scheme using ACO method for vehicular networks. J. Netw. Comput. Appl. **143**, 34–46 (2019)
32. Kennedy, J., Eberhart, R.: Particle swarm optimization (PSO). In: Proceedings of IEEE International Conference on Neural Networks, Perth, Australia (1995)
33. Saritha, V., Krishna, P.V., Misra, S., Obaidat, M.S.: Learning automata based optimized multipath routing using leapfrog algorithm for VANETs. In: 2017 IEEE International Conference on Communications (ICC), pp. 1–5, May 2017
34. Gupta, M., Sabharwal, N., Singla, P., Singh, J., Rodrigues, J.J.P.C.: PSARV: particle swarm angular routing in vehicular ad hoc networks. In: Woungang, I., Dhurandher, S.K. (eds.) WIDECOM 2018. LNDECT, vol. 27, pp. 115–127. Springer, Cham (2019). https://doi.org/10.1007/978-3-030-11437-4_9
35. Koç, E., Otri, S., Rahim, S., Pham, D.T., Ghanbarzadeh, A., Zaidi, M.: The bees algorithm–a novel tool for complex optimisation problems. In: Intelligent Production Machines and Systems, pp. 454–459. Elsevier (2006)
36. Zhang, X., Zhang, X.: A binary artificial bee colony algorithm for constructing spanning trees in vehicular ad hoc networks. Ad Hoc Netw. **58**, 198–204 (2017)
37. Kaur, S., Aseri, T.C., Rani, S.: QoS-aware routing in vehicular ad hoc networks using ant colony optimization and bee colony optimization. In: Krishna, C.R., Dutta, M., Kumar, R. (eds.) Proceedings of 2nd International Conference on Communication, Computing and Networking. LNNS, vol. 46, pp. 251–260. Springer, Singapore (2019). https://doi.org/10.1007/978-981-13-1217-5_25
38. Chu, S.-C., Tsai, P., Pan, J.-S.: Cat swarm optimization. In: Yang, Q., Webb, G. (eds.) PRICAI 2006. LNCS (LNAI), vol. 4099, pp. 854–858. Springer, Heidelberg (2006). https://doi.org/10.1007/978-3-540-36668-3_94
39. Kasana, R., Kumar, S.: A geographic routing algorithm based on cat swarm optimization for vehicular ad-hoc networks. In: 2017 4th International Conference on Signal Processing and Integrated Networks (SPIN), pp. 86–90, February 2017
40. Swagatam, D., Arijit, B., Sambarta, D., Ajith, A.: Bacterial foraging optimization algorithm: theoretical foundations, analysis, and applications. In: Abraham, A., Hassanien, A.E., Siarry, P., Engelbrecht, A. (eds.) Foundations of Computational Intelligence Volume 3, vol. 203, pp. 23–55. Springer, Heidelberg (2009). https://doi.org/10.1007/978-3-642-01085-9_2
41. Mehta, K., Bajaj, P.R., Malik, L.G.: Fuzzy bacterial foraging optimization zone based routing (fbfozbr) protocol for VANET. In: 2016 International Conference on ICT in Business Industry Government (ICTBIG), pp. 1–10, November 2016
42. Shattal, M.A., Wisniewska, A., Khan, B., Al-Fuqaha, A., Dombrowski, K.: From channel selection to strategy selection: enhancing vanets using socially-inspired foraging and deference strategies. IEEE Trans. Veh. Technol. **67**(9), 8919–8933 (2018)
43. Zheng, Y.-J.: Water wave optimization: a new nature-inspired metaheuristic. Comput. Oper. Res. **55**, 1–11 (2015)

44. Craik, A.D.D.: The origins of water wave theory. Annu. Rev. Fluid Mech. **36**, 1–28 (2004)
45. Wagh, M.B., Gomathi, N.: Water wave optimization-based routing protocol for vehicular adhoc networks. Int. J. Model. Simul. Sci. Comput. **9**(05), 1850047 (2018)
46. Mirjalili, S., Lewis, A.: The whale optimization algorithm. Adv. Eng. Softw. **95**, 51–67 (2016)
47. Valayapalayam Kittusamy, S.R., Elhoseny, M., Kathiresan, S.: An enhanced whale optimization algorithm for vehicular communication networks. Int. J. Commun. Syst. e3953 (2019)
48. Zadeh, L.A.: Fuzzy logic. Computer **21**(4), 83–93 (1988)
49. Alzamzami, O., Mahgoub, I.: Fuzzy logic-based geographic routing for urban vehicular networks using link quality and achievable throughput estimations. IEEE Trans. Intell. Transp. Syst. **20**(6), 2289–2300 (2019)
50. Fahad, T.O., Ali, A.A.: Compressed fuzzy logic based multi-criteria AODV routing in VANET environment. Int. J. Electr. Comput. Eng. (IJECE) **9**(1), 397–401 (2019)
51. Michie, D., Spiegelhalter, D.J., Taylor, C.C., et al.: Machine learning. Neural Stat. Classification **13**, 19–22 (1994)
52. Sutton, R.S., Barto, A.G., et al.: Introduction to Reinforcement Learning, vol. 2. MIT Press, Cambridge (1998)
53. Mammeri, Z.: Reinforcement learning based routing in networks: review and classification of approaches. IEEE Access **7**, 55916–55950 (2019)
54. Ji, X., et al.: Keep forwarding path freshest in VANET via applying reinforcement learning. In: 2019 IEEE First International Workshop on Network Meets Intelligent Computations (NMIC), pp. 13–18, July 2019
55. Jinqiao, W., Fang, M., Li, X.: Reinforcement learning based mobility adaptive routing for vehicular ad-hoc networks. Wirel. Pers. Commun. **101**(4), 2143–2171 (2018)
56. Sun, Y., Lin, Y., Tang, Y.: A reinforcement learning-based routing protocol in VANETs. In: Liang, Q., Mu, J., Jia, M., Wang, W., Feng, X., Zhang, B. (eds.) CSPS 2017. LNEE, vol. 463, pp. 2493–2500. Springer, Singapore (2019). https://doi.org/10.1007/978-981-10-6571-2_303
57. Hoang, D.T., Lu, X., Niyato, D., Wang, P., Kim, D.I., Han, Z.: Applications of repeated games in wireless networks: a survey. IEEE Commun. Surv. Tutor. **17**(4), 2102–2135 (2015)
58. Khan, A.A., Abolhasan, M., Ni, W.: An evolutionary game theoretic approach for stable and optimized clustering in VANETs. IEEE Trans. Veh. Technol. **67**(5), 4501–4513 (2018)
59. Wellington, L.J., Rosário, D., Cerqueira, E., Villas, L., Gerla, M.: A game theory approach for platoon-based driving for multimedia transmission in VANETs. Wirel. Commun. Mob. Comput. **2018**, 11 p. (2018)
60. Nunes, B.A.A., Mendonca, M., Nguyen, X., Obraczka, K., Turletti, T.: A survey of software-defined networking: past, present, and future of programmable networks. IEEE Commun. Surv. Tutor. **16**(3), 1617–1634 (2014)
61. Kreutz, D., Ramos, F.M.V., Veríssimo, P.E., Rothenberg, C.E., Azodolmolky, S., Uhlig, S.: Software-defined networking: a comprehensive survey. Proc. IEEE **103**(1), 14–76 (2015)
62. Jaballah, W.B., Conti, M., Lal, C.: A survey on software-defined VANETs: benefits, challenges, and future directions, April 2019

63. Ji, X., Yu, H., Fan, G., Fu, W.: SDGR: an SDN-based geographic routing proto-col for VANET. In: 2016 IEEE International Conference on Internet of Things (iThings) and IEEE Green Computing and Communications (GreenCom) and IEEE Cyber, Physical and Social Computing (CPSCom) and IEEE Smart Data (SmartData), pp. 276–281, December 2016

64. Rayeni, M.S., Hafid, A.: Routing in heterogeneous vehicular networks using an adapted software defined networking approach. In: 2018 Fifth International Con-ference on Software Defined Systems (SDS), pp. 25–31, April 2018

65. Kazmi, A., Khan, M.A., Akram, M.U.: DeVANET: Decentralized software-defined VANET architecture. In: 2016 IEEE International Conference on Cloud Engineer-ing Workshop (IC2EW), pp. 42–47, April 2016

66. Alioua, A., Senouci, S.-M., Moussaoui, S.: dSDiVN: a distributed software-defined networking architecture for infrastructure-less vehicular networks. In: Eichler, G., Erfurth, C., Fahrnberger, G. (eds.) I4CS 2017. CCIS, vol. 717, pp. 56–67. Springer, Cham (2017). https://doi.org/10.1007/978-3-319-60447-3_5

67. Hayes, B.: Cloud computing. Commun. ACM **51**(7), 9–11 (2008)

68. Bitam, S., Mellouk, A., Zeadally, S.: VANET-cloud: a generic cloud computing model for vehicular ad hoc networks. IEEE Wirel. Commun. **22**(1), 96–102 (2015)

69. Bhoi, S.K., Khilar, P.M.: RVCloud: a routing protocol for vehicular ad hoc network in city environment using cloud computing. Wirel. Netw. **22**(4), 96–102 (2016)

70. Olariu, S., Khalil, I., Abuelela, M.: Taking VANET to the clouds. Int. J. Pervasive Comput. Commun. **7**(1), 7–21 (2011)

71. Khalil, I., Mousannif, H., Olariu, S.: Cooperation as a service in VANET: imple-mentation and simulation results. Mob. Inf. Syst. **8**(2), 153–172 (2012)

72. Bonomi, F., Milito, R., Zhu, J., Addepalli, S.: Fog computing and its role in the Internet of Things. In: Proceedings of the First Edition of the MCC Workshop on Mobile Cloud Computing, pp. 13–16. ACM (2012)

73. Brennand, C.A.R.L., Boukerche, A., Meneguette, R., Villas, L.A.: A novel urban traffic management mechanism based on fog. In: 2017 IEEE Symposium on Com-puters and Communications (ISCC), pp. 377–382, July 2017

74. Hou, X., Li, Y., Chen, M., Di, W., Jin, D., Chen, S.: Vehicular fog computing: a viewpoint of vehicles as the infrastructures. IEEE Trans. Veh. Technol. **65**(6), 3860–3873 (2016)

75. Lu, T., Chang, S., Li, W.: Fog computing enabling geographic routing for urban area vehicular network. Peer-to-Peer Netw. Appl. **11**(4), 749–755 (2018)

76. Wu, C., Yoshinaga, T., Ji, Y., Zhang, Y.: Computational intelligence inspired data delivery for vehicle-to-roadside communications. IEEE Trans. Veh. Technol. **67**(12), 12038–12048 (2018)

77. Sun, G., Zhang, Y., Yu, H., Du, X., Guizani, M.: Intersection fog-based distributed routing for V2V communication in urban vehicular ad hoc networks. IEEE Trans. Intell. Transp. Syst. 1–14 (2019)

78. Tang, Y., Cheng, N., Wu, W., Wang, M., Dai, Y., Shen, X.: Delay-minimization routing for heterogeneous VANETs with machine learning based mobility predic-tion. IEEE Trans. Veh. Technol. **68**(4), 3967–3979 (2019)

79. Oubbati, O.S., Chaib, N., Lakas, A. and Bitam, S.: On-demand routing for urban VANETs using cooperating UAVs. In: 2018 International Conference on Smart Communications in Network Technologies (SaCoNeT), pp. 108–113, October 2018

A Systematic Literature Review of Studies on Road Congestion Modelling

Ahmed Derbel[✉] and Younes Boujelbene[✉]

FSEG of Sfax, Sfax University, 3018 Sfax, Tunisia
derbelamd@gmail.com, boujelbene.younes@yahoo.fr

Abstract. Congestion was one of the most serious global problems which create highly problematic social, economic and environmental conditions. In this regard, we have elaborated a systematic literature review study on the magnitudes of congestion that will attempt to answer this problem by presenting successively the causes of traffic congestion, the economic, societal and environmental issues, the solutions proposed to reduce road congestion and finally the actions to be taken for this purpose. In our pursuit of research, we have found that microscopic modeling has been used effectively to solve the most serious problems of road congestion through urban transportation system applications and road pricing policy. To the contrary, the macroscopic modeling applications are generally geared toward the achievement of long-term goals to alleviate road congestion through road traffic management and improved public transport.

Keywords: Traffic flow theory and modelling · Literature review · Measuring road congestion

1 Introduction

Around the world, traffic saturation leads to chronic congestion with numerous negative consequences in terms of aggravation, stress, lost time and environmental nuisance. Every year, we have billions of dollars to spend in the face of this phenomenon. The road congestion is also a major obstacle to the economic and social development in all of our cities and towns. Billions of hours are wasted every day in traffic jams and the quality of urban life is seriously affected by the continued growth of car traffic. Despite advances in vehicle technology, the growth of traffic and the discontinuous nature of driving in urban areas make cities a major and growing source of air pollution, climate change emissions, traffic noise and more efficient consumption of non-renewable resources. The traffic congestion is also an ongoing challenge for the development of a region and can result in terms of both direct and indirect costs linked to productivity losses, business activities and the free displacement of goods and people remain. We are indeed faced with a global problem similar in form and size. Understanding this problem has become a critical issue for all researchers and transport decision-makers. In this context, several researches have been carried out so far to reduce road traffic congestion and its economic, human and environmental consequences. As a result, we conducted a literature review based on the magnitude of road congestion. The objective of our research is to understand the causes of traffic jams, the solutions proposed to ease road-traffic congestion and finally the actions to be taken in worldwide transport

I. Jemili and M. Mosbah (Eds.): DiCES-N 2019, CCIS 1130, pp. 23–36, 2020.
https://doi.org/10.1007/978-3-030-40131-3_2

system. It will be presented successively the solutions that can be implemented in response to better manage transport demand. We also tried to answer all the most frequently asked questions in the traffic congestion analysis.

2 Research Methodology and Literature Review

The systematic review provided a synthesis of the scientific literature in response to find a global solution for the road traffic problems and to relieve road congestion in key corridors. We use explicit methods of searching, selecting, and analyzing data. The purpose of this systematic review is to locate relevant existing studies on the basis of a previously formulated research question, to evaluate and synthesize their respective contributions in this regard. Typically, systematic reviews have significant advantages over traditional narrative approaches in the literature reviews. These traditional journals generally do not follow a formal methodology, which leads to a lack of transparency and reproducibility. Systematic reviews represent powerful tools to identify, collect, synthesize, and evaluate primary research data on specific research questions in a highly standardized and reproducible manner. *"They enable the defensible synthesis of outcomes by increasing precision and minimizing bias whilst ensuring transparency of the methods used. This makes them especially valuable to inform evidence-based risk analysis and decision making in various topics and research disciplines"* [1]. Moreover, the quality of each included study is evaluated, so that the reader can decide on the reliability of the conclusions. Also in this case, statistical methods can be used to synthesize the results of the studies. We used statistical tools to improve the objectivity and validity of the results. This review article attempted to identify documents published in popular international journals and conferences. We extracted the most important information related to road traffic modeling and focused on the standard treatment of road congestion. As a result, we have sought to identify articles related to this issue in various parts of published articles such as keywords, title, research method, results, conclusions and discussion. The result of systematic reviews is shown in the Table 1 below. With regard to the classification system, a reference database system has been set up. It includes 25 articles published in more than 13 journals published and 12 proceeding papers from 2014 to 2019. The articles have been classified according to their authors, year of publication, name of the journal in which they were published, the techniques and approaches, case studies covering different regions around the world, the purpose of the study, the gaps and the problem of research, as well as the results illustrated in Table 1. Our research strategy has been a search for relevant studies in sources of scientific literature, represented by academic studies and has been published in peer-reviewed journals. We searched online databases to identify all articles published on the problem of congestion on the roads and traffic jam topics. The data has been searched from various sources (Scopus, ASCE library or IEEE Xplore digital library, Springer journals list) by applying different search filters, we only retained the papers that worked with a case study. The search was carried out using the Boolean operator 'AND' with the search terms 'congestion road' and 'traffic jam', and a second search with 'congestion during peak hours' as well as 'solution to traffic congestion'. Our data collection strategy is based primarily on computerized searches. We are aware that this involves focusing on newer articles in our data sweeps. This assumption is based on the fact that the most recent publications are often automatically indexed in computerized library systems. Subsequently, we defined exogenous variables and endogenous variables to develop an economic model as indicated in Fig. 1. The second step is to make a statistical analysis of the database. The objectives of the statistical analysis are used to evaluate a parameter, to determine whether a difference between two variables is due to chance or to a systematic cause, to evaluate the relationship between two variables. The choice of a statistical analysis method depends on the nature of the data. We worked with variables of the qualitative type, and for this reason we used two statistical techniques: the chi-square test and the multiple correspondence analyses (MCA). Finally, we used predictive statistical analysis using the neuron network to predict the situation, to measure the impact of exogenous variables on the endogenous variable and determine its margin of uncertainty.

Table 1. Presentation of the database architecture.

Model	Case-study	Level	Methodology of the study	Proposed solution	References
Macro	Beijing	Q2	Data mobility analysis	TM	[2]
Macro	Accra	Q2	Data mobility analysis	TM	[3]
Macro	Beijing	Q2	Spatiotemporal series	TM	[4]
Micro	Milan	Q2	Data mobility analysis	ITS	[5]
Macro	Asian cities	Q2	Data mobility analysis	RI	[6]
Macro	Rotterdam	Q3	Data mobility analysis	TM	[7]
Macro	Sfax	Q2	Byes model	TM	[8]
Macro	Budapest	Q3	Data mobility analysis	TM	[9]
Macro	Beijin	Q2	Data mobility analysis	TM	[10]
Macro	Kuala-Lumpur	Q2	Data mobility analysis	TM	[11]
Macro	Sao Paulo	Q1	Agent based model	TM	[12]
Macro	New Delhi	Q2	Dijkstra's algorithm	TM	[13]
Macro	Florida	Q1	Image processing	TM	[14]
Macro	Beijing	Q2	Data mobility analysis	TM	[15]
Macro	Boston	Q2	Flow Optimization	TM	[16]
Macro	Beijing	Q2	Data mobility analysis	TM	[17]
Macro	Dalian	Q2	Fuzzy mathematic	TM	[18]
Macro	Barcelona	Q2	Vehicle Routing	TM	[19]
Macro	Brisbane	Q2	Byes model	TM	[20]
Macro	Brisbane	Q2	Byes model	TM	[21]
Macro	Beijing	Q2	Byes model	TM	[22]
Micro	New York	Q2	Flow Optimization	RPS	[23]
Micro	California	Q3	Benchmark modeling	RPS	[24]
Macro	Jiangsu	Q2	Binary logistic model	PT	[25]
Macro	Poznań	Q3	Benchmark modeling	TM	[26]

RPS: Road pricing system, ITS: Intelligent Transportation Systems, RI: Road investment, PT: Public transportation, TM: Traffic management.

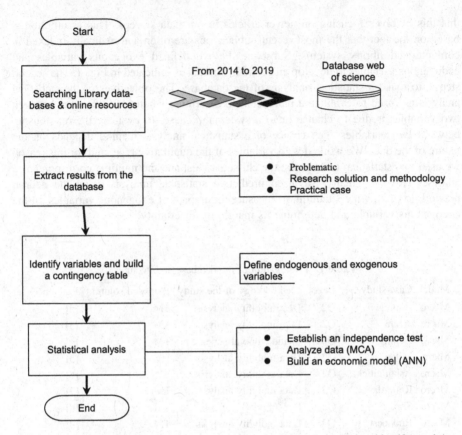

Fig. 1. The approach used for performing a systematic review. It is used to identify, evaluate, and synthesize scientific evidence that will answer all the questions about the magnitude of road congestion.

3 Endogenous Variable: Traffic Congestion Index

In the literature, measurement of travel time and delay are key elements to be considered in the determination of the congestion index. We chose two techniques to measure the index of road congestion. The first is based on the TomTom index, the TomTom website publishes each year a North American and a European index, an initiative launched in 2007 to reveal, quantify and compare road traffic in major cities. In addition, the INRIX index allows us to give a clear view of the quality of congestion, especially in congested cities in Asia. All TomTom[1] and INRIX[2] index used by motorists provide the company's servers with anonymous data on the position, speed and direction of each vehicle. The decision makers and transport planners can therefore

---

[1] https://www.tomtom.com/en_gb/traffic-index/ranking/.

[2] http://inrix.com/scorecard/.

average normal speed for each street, compare with the maximum speed allowed, detect slowdowns and traffic jams and calculate how much time is lost per day, month and year on each major city's roads. The comparison between the cities was established by a congestion score as well as by the congestion level (Q1: very high degree of congestion, Q2: intense congestion, Q3: low congestion and Q4: no congestion or light congestion) and the type of roadway chosen for the given trip.

4 Exogenous Variables

4.1 Traffic Modeling

Depending on the global road network or the local interactions between a few vehicles when changing direction or approaching an intersection, the question of choosing the right model and architecture is paramount. Generally, there are two types of observable phenomena that correspond to two distinct approaches. First, the local phenomena that involve a small number of vehicles and only extend a few tens of meters. For example, highway exit, the regulation of a traffic intersection, etc. On the other hand, there are global phenomena that target a large number of vehicles and extend over a very wide temporal and spatial dimension. It seems natural to consider a microscopic scale in the first situation while the second requires a macroscopic representation.

Microscopic Modeling: It is a model that describes the behavior and individual interactions of each driver in a traffic system. The first researches of the microscopic simulation of the road traffic were oriented on the behavior of the vehicle in a circulation environment. To model the trajectories of individual vehicles, we classically distinguished two classes of behavior. The pursuit behaviors that describe the adaptation of vehicles with their position, speed or acceleration according to the surrounding vehicles. The lane change model illustrates how vehicles change lanes (overtaking and turning conditions, changing lanes, etc.). The analysis of driver behavior is based on the following principle: the driver perceives a stimulus at time (t) and reacts with a certain reaction time (Tr). The reaction is proportional to the intensity of the stimulus and depends on the sensitivity of the driver in relation to this stimulus.

$$\text{response time } (t + Tr) = \text{sensitivity} * \text{stimulus} \tag{1}$$

Macroscopic Models: The macroscopic models describe traffic at a high level of aggregation to repeatedly generate vehicle flows regardless of the component parts. These models are typically used for planning and control operations on large networks. The description of a vehicle flow is mainly done using three variables: the speed v (km/h or m/s), the density (or concentration) K (vehicles/km) and the flow Q (vehicles/h). It is represented by a hyperbolic equation connecting speed to the spatial density of vehicles. Typical vehicle maneuvers, such as lane changes and individual motion analyzes, cannot be represented in the macroscopic model. The purpose of this model is used to plan and control vehicle flows at a relatively large scale of the study.

The macroscopic models are based on the analogy with fluid dynamics and are more appropriate control laws to simulate a road flow over a large network. The macroscopic model has been used in several cities to solve road congestion problems, to measure infrastructure capacity and to improve the management of traffic flows and journeys. However, three models are the most recognized today in the literature to represent the dynamics of traffic at the macroscopic level: the LWR equilibrium model, the ARZ non-equilibrium model, and the MOD original-destination multi-class model. Finally, the simplest classical version derives from a physical principle expressed by the following conservation equation.

$$\begin{cases} Q(x,t) = K(x,t) \times V(x,t) \\ \dfrac{\partial Q(x,t)}{\partial x} + \dfrac{\partial K(x,t)}{\partial t} = 0 \end{cases} \qquad (2)$$

4.2 Congestion Management Solutions

In the literature, there is often an impressive range of possible solutions that correspond not only to improvements in road capacity, but also to reducing the demand for road traffic. Subsequently, the public authority should take into account road transportation alternatives, including other non-road modes in their search for possible solutions. Although extended, the development of non-road transportation modes also contributes to overcoming congestion in the road network. The creation of tram lines, transport on rails can classify as possible alternatives to cushion the impact of the traffic congestion. Alternative modes of transport (walking, cycling) are other recent solutions used in central areas to limit the negative externalities of urban road transport. In the following, we presented the different possible solutions that can fight against this situation.

Road Pricing System (RPS): Among the instruments linked to congestion pricing, tolls can be very precisely applied to avoid congestion on road sections with very high traffic density. Transportation decision-makers can take strict steps imposing toll congestion pricing for all travelers that is within urban areas. The regulation toll may vary depending on the time slots (it started to increase in function of the traffic density), depending on the type of vehicle (truck, car, motorcycle), depending on the time and the day of access to critical situations (rush hour, holidays and weekends). This technique should be linked to en-route traffic demand and to allow the free flow in all directions without any congestion or blocking.

Intelligent Transportation Systems (ITS): Historically, ITS appeared in the 1990 s, and it can be defined as the integrated application of advanced sensors between vehicles and infrastructure. As a result, advanced data processing has witnessed tremendous efforts to create and deploy a new generation of the road transport system with the goal of increasing mobility, minimizing environmental impact, improving efficiency and promote the efficiency of private and public fleets [27]. Technology based approaches include a variety of measures likely to improve the management of transport systems in general and road capacity in particular. ITS offers a wide range of options to act on both supply and demand sides. The systems take into account the dynamic interaction between all components of a transportation system: the passenger, the driver, the vehicle the infrastructure, and driving assistance system [28].

Road Investment (RI): Lack of investment in road infrastructure is one of the main causes of increased congestion. The limited capacity of road infrastructures is a source of significant nuisance, involving the destruction of economic, social and environmental well-being, particularly in areas close to urban agglomerations (where travel is often concentrated). The construction of new roads and the improvement of existing roads should meet high standards from an environmental and aesthetic point of view. Investments in high quality infrastructure increase traffic speed and ensure a flow of traffic at reasonable levels of service. In majority case, building new roads (repaired and rebuilt) is very expensive because the transportation investments need to be made over many years and are very costly. Furthermore, several studies have shown that the creation of new roads or the extension of existing roads can lead to congestion. This is the famous paradox of Brass, the construction of a new space can temporarily increase the speed of circulation, but generally leads to lower operational reliability (the volume of the traffic increases in parallel to fill this space).

Public Transportation (PT): Most experiences around the world show that the best way to reduce car traffic during peak hours is not to increase the number of lanes on motorways, but to develop alternative modes of transport and to promote urban diversity [29]. For many years, a multitude of analyzes, impact studies and reports published around the world have recognized the benefits of public transit for the quality of life of the population. Governments and the majority of socio-economic actors recognize that public transit contributes to the rational use of energy and the reduction of greenhouse gas emissions and air contaminants. The implementation of preferential measures for buses makes it possible to increase these advantages and allows a significant reduction of the road congestion thanks to the modal transfer [30].

Traffic Management (TM): Traffic management systems participate fully in the management of road traffic through the dynamic means and equipment used by the PC traffic on the road and motorway networks. They are also a major asset for the information of users and more generally for the operation and maintenance of the road. On motorways and urban expressways, as traffic intensifies, and to avoid the formation of congestion, the managers operate a set of measures to balance the supply (capacity of the infrastructure to sell the traffic) with the traffic request. In the field, road traffic management research makes it possible to perform: the collection of data (electromagnetic loops installed on the roadway, infrared detectors, DSRC antenna, etc.), traffic monitoring and information system (cameras), the dissemination of information or instructions to users (variable message signs, the communication between the equipment and the traffic PC (optical fiber, ADSL, etc.).

5 Empirical Part

The empirical part was divided into three parts, the chi-square test, multiple correspondence analysis and the application of a neuron network.

5.1   Chi-Square Analysis for Attribute Data

The Chi-square is used to test the dependency relationship between two categorical variables. We can also say that this test verifies the hypothesis of independence of these variables. If two variables depend on each other, they share similarities and interactions, the variation of one can be influenced by the variation of the other. As we are going to work with categorical variables, we are not going to use the average or variance as a reference. It would be irrelevant to calculate the average of a categorical variable, the average obtained would be depend on the number of observations in each category. Therefore, we will rather work with the frequencies (or even the occurrences or the proportions) obtained in each cell of the pivot table. We also found that there is an extremely strong economic link between road traffic modeling and research solution to traffic congestion problems (p-value < 0.05), representing the same information quantity to explain road congestion. On the other hand, the relation between (solutions and the research methodology) and the relation between (the road traffic modeling and the research methodology) are mutually independent variables. This implies that both variables are of great importance to explain road traffic congestion (p-value > 0.05), as indicated in Table 2.

Table 2. The results of the Chi-Square test

Traffic modeling and methodology		Solutions and traffic modeling		Solutions and methodology	
Khi^2 (Observed value)	7,386	Khi^2 (Observed value)	26	Khi^2 (Observed value)	34,9
Khi^2 (Critical value)	18,30	Khi^2 (Critical value)	9,48	Khi^2 (Critical value)	55,7
DDL	10	DDL	4	DDL	40
p-value	0,051	p-value	0,001	p-value	0,6

5.2   Multiple Correspondence Analysis

There are several factors analysis techniques, the most common of which are Principal Component Analysis (PCA) for quantitative variables, Correspondence Factor Analysis (CFA) for two qualitative variables, and multiple correspondence analysis (MCA) on several qualitative variables (this is an extension of the CFA). Multiple correspondence analysis is a descriptive technique that summarizes the information contained in a large number of variables in order to facilitate the interpretation of existing correlations between these variables. The general idea is this. The set of individuals can be represented in a multi-dimensional space where each axis represents the different variables used to describe each individual. Thus it takes two or three axes to describe a variable with 25 articles research. Individuals will then be projected and represented on a new axis system. This new system of axes is chosen in such a way that the majority of the variations is concentrated on the first axes. The first two or three axes will explain the majority of the differences observed in the sample, the other axes providing only a small additional piece of information. Therefore, the analysis can concentrate on its first axes which will constitute a good summary of the observed variations in the sample.

We have found that microscopic modeling has been used effectively to solve the most serious problems of road congestion through urban transportation system applications and road pricing policy, as illustrated in references R4, R22 and R23. Macroscopic modeling is practically in a negative correlation (negative scalar product) compared to microscopic modeling. Moreover, macroscopic modeling applications are generally geared toward the achievement of long-term goals to alleviate road congestion through road traffic management and improved public transport. In addition, macroscopic modeling has been applied to reduce congestion through investments in transportation infrastructure and when the congestion situation is in the second degree (Q2). On the other hand, improvements in public transport services were used when the congestion situation is moderately fluid (Q3), as illustrated with references R25, R8 and R24, as indicated in Fig. 2. Public transportation is a key element in reducing traffic congestion, which means that the reduction of traffic congestion in the major cities is passed by improving public transit services, promoting cycling and walking, as well as to limiting the growth of private car. The improvement of public transport services is a first preventive step in the fight against urban congestion. We have also noticed that the improvement of the public transport network is a subject in its own right and does not depend on either macroscopic or microscopic modeling.

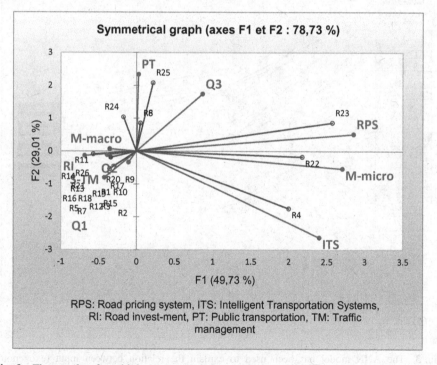

Fig. 2. The result of multiple correspondence analysis. Multiple correspondence analysis quantifies nominal (categorical) data by presenting the contingency table with a graph.

5.3 Artificial Neural Network

The technique of artificial neural networks (ANN) is a modeling tool that has now been proven in many fields (banking, military, meteorological, etc.) in response to problems as diverse as those relating to forecasting, classification, or still the signal processing. It is also based on its ability to learn by example, and extract from a sample of data, the physical phenomenon to model. The networks of multilayer neurons may comprise millions of neurons, distributed in several tens of layers. They are used in deep learning to design supervised and unsupervised learning mechanisms. The growing success of neural networks in most other statistical techniques can be attributed to their quality of its results in terms of precision and availability, versatility and it has an easy to implement and use interface. Neural networks are extremely sophisticated modeling and forecasting techniques, able to model relationships between data or particularly complex functions.

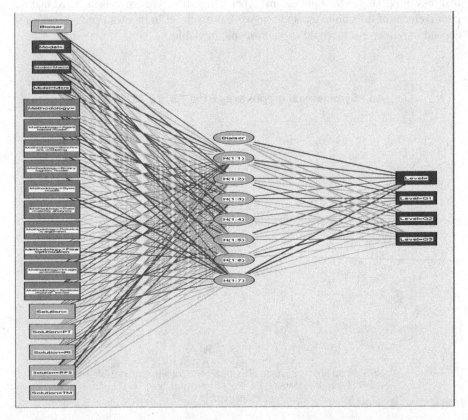

Fig. 3. The ANN model has been used to explain the relation between input (exogenous variables) and output (endogenous variable)

The modeling of the phenomenon of road congestion in the neural network goes through a first phase called learning phase. In the most frequent case, input vectors are presented to the network for adjusting the weighting of each neuron, and are in place to bring about the desired output as close as possible to those calculated. In predictive statistics, we used the ANN to explain and predict the endogenous variable based on exogenous variables, as illustrated in Fig. 3. From the confusion matrix, the ANN showed great accuracy in predicting the congestion situation compared to other prediction methods. This model performs well against logistic regression and SVM, as indicated in Table 3 below.

Table 3. Model evaluation of output data

Method	AUC	F1	Precision	Recall
SVM	0.108	0.917	0.910	0.923
Neural network	0.950	0.937	0.930	0.952
Logistic regression	0.883	0.815	0.872	0.846

We also found that the research methodology is the most relevant and significant variable to explain the congestion situation compared to other exogenous variables (It has the highest value of information gain, gain ratio and score of chi-square). This implies that the research methodology is of great importance for the problem of congestion that we have the duty to elaborate, as indicated in Table 4 below. The methodology has had a considerable impact on congestion and pollution. In fact, when the authors tend to deal with the problem of congestion, the researchers need to determine their own priorities and to find mitigation solutions could in fact be able to solve the serious problem of urban congestion. Generally, economic models have been used to anticipate the risk of congestion in the context of macroscopic modeling and to analyze road traffic situations. On the other hand, microscopic analysis has been used to express congestion on a very small scale in the case of tolls or intelligent transportation system applications.

Table 4. Evaluation of input data

Exogenous variables	Info. gain	Gain ratio	Chi-Square
Methodology	0.502	0.173	2.63
Congestion management solutions	0.07	0.057	0.00
Traffic modeling	0.005	0.010	0.001

6   Discussion and Conclusion

Generally, the suggestion that congestion should be minimized is questionable or indeterminate sign. There is no single, feasible solution to designing and implementing a transportation system that would not experience congestion. All the possible and conceivable solutions were created advantages on the plane of displacement, but also they gave disadvantages in other planes (financial, economic and social). We also felt that the level of zero congestion cannot technically be achieved and that there is no quick fix or easy to build. The construction of new road, the installation of TCSP, the restriction the use of the vehicle can improve a little the mobility but not to revolutionize it. Financial constraints remain a decisive factor in planning. There is a need to encourage public debate on innovative solutions to congestion, including transit expansion, congestion pricing, transportation demand management, and more. In addition, citizen training and education can increase opportunities to change their driving behavior and reduce traffic congestion through good traffic maneuvering. The congestion solution is not only technological, but also and above all of a human nature. Finally, it is time to focus on education, awareness and training drivers to become the real players of road traffic.

6.1   The Sustainable Development of Mobility and Public Transportation

We can classify the solutions explored into two broad categories. Initiatives such as the restriction of vehicle use, ITS, pricing system and investment in infrastructure are included in the procedure of road traffic management and these terms are directly related to the traffic theory. These instructions are complementary and interdependent with each other. The objectives of this policy are to streamline the flow of traffic during peak demand periods and when the road temporarily loses some of its capacity. The improvement of public transport efficiency is introduced under the notion of the performance of public transport services. Public transport is a key instrument for mobility management that can contribute to the satisfaction of many community needs. Improvements in the performance of public transport operators can cause an increase in the total number of passengers, and public transport becomes more and more attractive compared to the use of the private car [31].

6.2   Relationship Between Congestion and Road Traffic Modeling

We studied the theory of traffic flow in order to specify the different types of modeling. Traffic modeling seeks to provide a simplified representation of a complex situation to allow a better understanding of the links between road traffic variables. This is an important issue for the development of traffic networks and the optimization of transport infrastructure. As much in practice as in theory, we presented two types of modeling (macroscopic modeling and microscopic modeling). Microscopic modeling involves an individual presentation of vehicles and macroscopic modeling involves an overall presentation of traffic flows. First of all, remember that each model has its own limits of representation, each type of model is presented by a particular framework of use, it is very difficult to be able to apply a model from different directions (the results are disappointing because the model is unsuitable). For example, it seems quite inappropriate to use a macroscopic model in a very fine network, since it will be very difficult to judge the relevance of macroscopic indicators such as concentration (respectively flow), and the he length of time concerned is very limited (respectively the aggregation period). However, before any study on road traffic can be done, it is necessary to specify the spatial and temporal scales of this study. This choice is sometimes made according to the means (data of pre-existing measurements, material means of measurement, etc.) and mainly on the scales which adapt according to the objectives pursued. Microscopic models are often used for offline simulation to test the new infrastructure (entry/ exit ramps, lane removal, etc.), new automotive equipment (driver assistance system), or have a rough idea about flow data difficult to compute empirically. The application of microscopic models in the real time regulation of the flow is very limited given the enormous computing times they require and the absence of an explicit model describing the relationship between the input/output data.

In the case of the application of limit values, the number of observations used to do the systematic review is very limited. In the next search, we will realize an expanded database in order to conduct a more comprehensive study, and to include all cases in traffic congestion around the world.

References

1. Kohl, C., et al.: Can systematic reviews inform GMO risk assessment and risk management? (2015). https://doi.org/10.3389/fbioe.2015.00113
2. Feifei, H., YanYang, L.: Traffic congestion assessment method for urban road networks based on speed performance index. Procedia Eng. **137**, 425–433 (2016)
3. Frances, A., Thomas, K.: Traffic congestion in the Accra Central Market, Ghana. J. Urban Manag. **7**(2), 85–96 (2018)
4. Limiao, Z., Guanwen, Z., Daqing, L., Hai-Jun, H., Harry, E., Shlomo, H.: Scale-free resilience of real traffic JAMS. In: Proceedings of the National Academy of Sciences (2018). https://doi.org/10.1073/pnas.1814982116
5. Albert, S., Sergio, G., Alex, A.: A model to identify urban traffic congestion hotspots in complex networks. R. Soc. **3**(10) (2016). http://doi.org/10.1098/rsos.160098
6. Liang, W., Jeff, K., Xiumei, G., Dora, M.: Solving traffic congestion through street renaissance: a perspective from dense asian cities. Urban Sci. Spec. Issue Sustain. Place Mak. Urban Gov. (2018). https://doi.org/10.3390/urbansci3010018
7. Guangyang, H., Suren, C., Yan, H.: Traffic performance assessment methodology of degraded roadway links following hazards. J. Aerosp. Eng. **32**(5), 04019055 (2019)
8. Derbel, A., Boujelbene, Y.: Road congestion analysis in the agglomeration of Sfax using a Bayesian model. In: Boudriga, N., Alouini, M.-S., Rekhis, S., Sabir, E., Pollin, S. (eds.) UNet 2018. LNCS, vol. 11277, pp. 131–142. Springer, Cham (2018). https://doi.org/10.1007/978-3-030-02849-7_12
9. Baji, P.: Using Google Maps road traffic estimations to unfold spatial and temporal inequalities of urban road congestion. Hung. Geogr. Bull. **67**(1), 61–74 (2018)
10. Pengcheng, J., Lei, L., Lizhen, C., Hui, L., Yuliang, S.: Congestion prediction of urban traffic employing SRBDP. In: IEEE International Symposium on Parallel and Distributed Processing with Applications and IEEE International Conference on Ubiquitous Computing and Communications (2017)
11. Saargunawathy, M., Muhammad, A., Kamaludin, M., Ramdhan, S.: Analysis of vehicular traffic flow in the major areas of Kuala Lumpur utilizing open-traffic. In: AIP Conference Proceedings, vol. 1883 (2017)
12. Weka, I., Ade, S., Russ, B. Febri, Z.: Developing model of toll road traffic forecasting during ramp-up period. In: The 2nd Conference for Civil Engineering Research Networks, vol 270 (2019)

13. Pattanaik, V., Singh, M., Gupta, P.K., Singh, S.K.: Smart real-time traffic congestion estimation and clustering technique for urban vehicular roads. In: IEEE Region 10 Conference (TENCON), Singapore, pp. 3420–3423 (2016). https://doi.org/10.1109/tencon.2016.7848689
14. Petrovska, N., Stevanovic, A.: Traffic congestion analysis visualisation tool. In: 18th International Conference on Intelligent Transportation Systems, Las Palmas, pp. 1489–1494 (2015). https://doi.org/10.1109/itsc.2015.243
15. Huimin, W., Jianping, S.: Study on traffic congestion patterns of large city in China taking Beijing as an example. Procedia - Soc. Behav. Sci. **138**(14), 482–491 (2014)
16. Junjie, W., Dong, W., Kun, H., Hang, G., Wang, P.: Encapsulating urban traffic rhythms into road networks. Sci. Rep. **4**, 4141 (2014)
17. Wang, J., Mao, Y., Li, J., Xiong, Z., Wang, W.-X.: Predictability of road traffic and congestion in urban areas. PLoS ONE **10**(4), e0121825 (2015). https://doi.org/10.1371/journal.pone.0121825
18. Wang, W.-X., Guo, R.-J.: Research on road traffic congestion index based on comprehensive parameters: taking Dalian city as an example. Adv. Mech. Eng. (2018). https://doi.org/10.1177/1687814018781482
19. Pablo, A., Iosu, L., Adrian, S., Javier, F.: The impact of traffic congestion when optimising delivery routes in real time. a case study in Spain. Int. J. Logist. Res. Appl. **21**(5), 529–541 (2018). https://doi.org/10.1080/13675567.2018.1457634
20. Wang, G., Kim, J.: The prediction of traffic congestion and incident on urban road networks using Naive Bayes classifier. In: Australasian Transport Research Forum Proceedings (2016)
21. Kim, J., Wang, G.: Diagnosis and prediction of traffic congestion on urban road networks using Bayesian networks. Transp. Res. Rec. J. Transp. Res. Board **2595**, 108–118 (2016)
22. YiLiu, X., Quan, W., Hemeizi, Z., Xinye, W.: Prediction of urban road congestion using a Bayesian network approach. Procedia - Soc. Behav. Sci. **138**(14), 671–678 (2014)
23. Mauro, S., Federico, R., Maximilian, S., Christopher, H., Marco, P.: On the interaction between autonomous mobility-on-demand and public transportation systems. Comput. Sci.: Syst. Control (2018)
24. Justin, B., Hossein, F., Cynthia, L.: Public transit investment and sustainable transportation: a review of studies of transit's impact on traffic congestion and air quality. Res. Transp. Econ. **52**, 15–22 (2015)
25. Ranran, Y., Ruyin, L.: Analysis of the influencing factors of the public willingness to participate in public bicycle projects and intervention strategies—a case study of Jiangsu Province, China. Sustain. MDPI Open Access J. **8**(4), 1–16 (2016)
26. Łukasz, O., Jacek, Ż.: Design of passenger public transportation solutions based on autonomous vehicles and their multiple criteria comparison with traditional forms of passenger transportation. Transp. Res. Procedia **10**, 472–482 (2015)
27. Derbel, A., Boujelbene, Y.: Development an approach to fusion of an anti-collision system. In: International Conference on Advanced Logistics and Transport (ICALT) (2014). https://doi.org/10.1109/ICAdLT.2014.6864080
28. Derbel, A., Boujelbene, Y.: Bayesian network for traffic management application: estimated the travel time. In: 2015 2nd World Symposium on Web Applications and Networking (WSWAN), Sousse, pp. 1–6 (2015). https://doi.org/10.1109/wswan.2015.7210328
29. Boujelbene, Y., Derbel, A.: The performance analysis of public transport operators in Tunisia using AHP method. Procedia Comput. Sci. **73**, 498–508 (2015)
30. Boujelbene, Y., Derbel, A.: The performance analysis of public transport operators in Tunisia using ER approach. Glob. J. Manag. Bus. Res. **16**(1) (2016)
31. Derbel, A., Boujelbene, Y.: Automatic classification and analysis of multiple-criteria decision making. In: Bouhlel, M.S., Rovetta, S. (eds.) SETIT 2018. SIST, vol. 146, pp. 83–93. Springer, Cham (2020). https://doi.org/10.1007/978-3-030-21005-2_8

A Comparative Study of Vehicle Detection Methods in a Video Sequence

Ameni Chetouane[1(✉)], Sabra Mabrouk[1], Imen Jemili[1], and Mohamed Mosbah[2]

[1] Faculty of sciences of Bizerte, University of Carthage, Tunis, Tunisia
{ameni.chetouane,sabra.mabrouk,imen.jmili}@fsb.u-carthage.tn
[2] University of Bordeaux, Bordeaux, France
mohamed.mosbah@u-bordeaux.fr

Abstract. Vehicle detection plays a significant role in traffic monitoring. Vehicle detection approaches can be used for vehicle tracking, vehicle classification and traffic analysis. However, numerous attributes like shape, intensity, size, pose, illumination, shadows, occlusion, velocity of vehicles and environmental conditions, provide different challenges for the detection step. With an appropriate vehicle detection technique, we are able to extract valuable knowledge from video sequences, regardless these diverse factors. Since the vehicle detection method choice has a deep impact on this step and the whole traffic monitoring system performances, our objective in this study is to investigate different methods for vehicle detection. Comparison is made on the basis of different metrics such as recall, precision and detection accuracy. These approaches have been tested under different weather conditions (rainy, sunny) and various traffic conditions (light, medium, heavy).

Keywords: Traffic monitoring · Vehicle detection · Aggregate Channel Features · Optical flow · Gaussian mixture model

1 Introduction

In up growing cities, due to rising population and expanding urbanization, the increased number of vehicles leads to traffic delay and overcrowding, especially in peak hours. The road congestion is considered as a veritable scourge, not only for drivers, but also for pedestrians, motorists, users of public transport, etc. Through the deployment of Intelligent transport systems (ITS), the authorities try to solve these various road traffic issues [11,26,33]. In this context, the recourse to visual traffic surveillance is an attractive and cost-effective solution, since cameras are cheaper and provide high quality video sequence [10,21].

Regardless the method category, numerous attributes like shape, intensity, size, pose, illumination, shadows, occlusion, velocity of vehicles and environmental conditions, provide different challenges for the detection step. With an appropriate vehicle detection technique, we are able to extract valuable knowledge from video sequences. This research work investigates techniques for vision

© Springer Nature Switzerland AG 2020
I. Jemili and M. Mosbah (Eds.): DiCES-N 2019, CCIS 1130, pp. 37–53, 2020.
https://doi.org/10.1007/978-3-030-40131-3_3

based vehicle detection. More specifically, we are interested in vehicles detection while taking into account diverse lightning conditions majorly sequences in sunlight and rain and further handling the occlusion.

In literature, various comprehensive reviews of different approaches for vehicle detection have been presented. On board vehicle detection has attracted many attention, as low-cost cameras are able to identify the color, shape and size of a moving object, even in high speed. In [47], the authors presented a review of on-road vehicle detection, while considering cameras mounted in vehicles. For to the two steps of vehicle detection, the authors classify state of the art approaches into subcategories such as knowledge, stereo vision, motion and appearance based methods. The different approaches are discussed and evaluated for a potential future deployment. A different classification is adopted in [43] where the authors presented a review of vision-based vehicle detection in both monocular and stereo vision.

Other researches using cameras configured on roadside have been proposed for years [24, 32, 44, 51, 55].

In [16], an overview of motion and appearance based methods for vehicle detection on a video traffic scene using a fixed mono camera is presented with a comparative study of different approaches. Authors conclude about the effectiveness of the deep learning based method. Similarly, several other papers provided a review of literature on vehicle detection, recognition and tracking methods with, in particular, appearance and motion based models [27, 42]. In [22], authors present a short and synthetic review of vehicle type classification methods besides vehicle detection ones, they identify problems mainly related to data classification such as similar size and shape of vehicles. This ascertainment was also addressed in [1] as an open research area. Authors in this paper recommend combining the studied methodologies to enhance vehicle classification results and to include more broad semantic characteristics.

In this paper, we present an experimental study assessing the performance of different vehicle detection techniques in order to select the most suitable one for traffic analysis. We use dataset including video sequences from cameras fixed on the bridge of Bizerte. These sequences contain typical challenges such as various weather conditions, different lighting conditions and image blurring.

The paper is organized as follows: Sect. 2 deals with the related work. Section 3 details the studied methods. The experimental study with its results are presented in Sect. 4. Finally, Sect. 5 gives the conclusion.

2 Related Work

The research community has proposed strong and generic methods able to reliably detect and track on-road vehicles in real time, over extended periods, in various climatic conditions and complicated urban traffic scenes.

The vehicle detection methods can be divided into the following categories:

2.1 Appearance-Based Approaches

Appearance-based approaches recognize vehicles from images, they use features such as shape, color and vehicles size. In [48], the authors proposed a vehicle detection method from static images using color and edges. This method can recognize vehicles without motion information, allowing slowly moving vehicles to be correctly detected from image sequences. Moreover, this approach is only useful and efficient in daylight with acceptable ambient illuminations.

Through the years, these simpler image features have been replaced by more general and robust feature sets for vehicle detection, such as Histogram of oriented gradient (HOG) features and Haar-like features which are well represented in the vehicle detection literature [13,29]. In [14], vehicles are first detected using Haar-like features, as they require a relatively limited training data. Then, an adaptive appearance-based model is built to dynamically track detected vehicles. In [28], the authors proposed a method based on the scale-invariant feature transform (SIFT) features [31] and boosting classifier [6]. This approach presents acceptable results, however, it is unsuitable for real-time applications. Authors in [34], tackled vehicle detection and tracking using an efficient background cancellation technique and Haar-like features with a modified Adaboost. In [8], the authors proposed an infrared image vehicle detection algorithm based on Haar-like features.

These latter features were used in several other researches in combination with different classifiers, such in [12] where Choudhury et al. suggested a method for vehicle detection based on Haar-like feature and the Adaboost classifier. In [53], the authors used firstly Haar like features to detect the region of interest of the candidate vehicle and then a combination of the Histogram of Oriented Gradients (HOG) and the Support Vector Machine (SVM) classifier was applied to precisely delimit the vehicle in the previously detected region of interest. The detection accuracy and the computation time were improved but this method is very depending on first step results.

2.2 Motion-Based Approaches

Motion based methods require a sequence of images to recognize vehicles. These approaches are less common than appearance-based methods. In order to cope with the dynamic of on-road environment, adaptive background models have been employed in several studies.

In [41], the authors used a background subtraction algorithm to detect vehicle based on blocks then a deep learning data validation algorithm is used. In [7], vehicles are detected using a machine learning based background subtraction approach having as features high-order statistics of the grayscale images. Authors proved the robustness of the method to illumination inhomogeneity and the effectiveness of the artificial neural network (ANN) method over Naive Bayes and K-Nearest Neighbours models in particular. The authors in [25], evaluated three background-modeling approaches for vehicle detection in highway traffic

videos. They present an objective comparison allowing to select the most suitable algorithm based on their data and conditions. In order to track moving
objects, Shukla and Sani [39] suggested a method based on frame differencing
and trajectory of motion. The main problem of this method is the increasing of
false negatives in generated foreground.

Optical flow has been also used in several studies. In [54], authors proposed
to detect overtaking vehicles allowing to assist drivers for a safe lane change.
They detected candidate vehicles based on motion cues, these moving objects
are then identified using Convolutional Neural Network (CNN) and tracked for
behaviour analysis in a short period of time. The Optical Flow Density algorithm
was applied in [45] to detect vehicles using the gradient of object displacement on
video frames. It was combined with Hungarian Kalman filter (HKF) for tracking
and Single line counting for vehicle counting. The authors present promising
accuracy rates in various conditions like shadow, illumination change, weather,
blur due to motion.

Motion-based approaches are appropriate for real time systems and detection
rate is usually satisfying as the majority of moving regions can be easily detected.
Yet, these approaches generally consider only the motion of vehicles and neglect
any other vehicle feature and can be affected by illumination changes. In [56],
the authors assume that "motion-based methods are sensitive to noise and can
typically achieve a high rate of false alarms".

2.3   Object-Based Approaches

An object-based approach requires three steps in order to detect the vehicles:
segmentation, training and validation. Depending on the number of frames, the
first step takes some training images from the total number of images. Then,
it proceeds with the segmentation parameters optimization. Finally, validation is operated on test samples to measure accuracy. Many approaches rely
on different learning-based object detectors like Aggregate Channel Features
(ACF) [5], Region-Based Convolutional Neural Network (RCNN) [18], FastR-
CNN [17], FasterRCNN [37] and You Only Look Once (YOLO) [36].

- RCNN: RCNN detection algorithm aims to identify and classify the main
  objects in the image. Initially, the R-CNN detector produces candidate regions
  using selective search [49] and then extracts, from each region, feature vectors
  using CNN. Later, the support vector machine (SVM) classifies the object in
  the candidate regions [18]. RCNN performed well, but it is very slow as it
  requires CNN feature map computation for every proposal obtained from the
  selective search.
- FastRCNN: Having an image and a set of object proposals as input, the FastRCNN proceed with two steps; region proposal and object recognition. It
  begins by processing multiple convolutional and max-pooling layers on the
  image and the region of interest (ROI) pooling layer converts the features
  inside valid region of interest into a fixed-size feature map for each region proposal. These features are then transformed to feature vector that are routed

to a fully connected layers. Every ROI generate two output vectors; softmax probabilities and four real-value numbers for each of the object classes. These four numbers refer to the bounding box position for one of the classes. Compared to R-CNN, Fast R-CNN offers one-step training with a higher average accuracy, which updates all network layers. In [20], the authors propose a simplified Fast R-CNN where the object recognition step is dropped and the region proposal is specified as vehicle proposal.

– FasterRCNN: In order to extract the regions proposal, Faster R-CNN uses a deep convolutional network. It changes selective search with a region proposal network (RPN) which employs Anchor Boxes to detect object and generates an output of rectangular object proposals. Region proposals process in Faster R-CNN is faster and ensures precise object detection.

– YOLO: While all of the preceding object detection algorithms employ regions to locate the object within the image, YOLO is based on regression where the classes and bounding boxes for the whole image are predicted in one run of the algorithm instead of selecting regions of interest.

3   Vehicle Detection Method

In the literature, various methods for vehicle detection have been presented. In our paper, we have used three methods, namely Gaussian mixture model and blob analysis, optical flow and blob analysis and the ACF object detector.

3.1   Gaussian Mixture Model

3.1.1   Gaussian Mixture Model Background

In [46], the authors proposed to model each pixel as a mixture of K gaussians (K usually varies between 3 and 5). The probability distribution at a pixel X_t is described as follows:

$$P(X_t) = \sum_{i=1}^{K} \omega_{i,t} * \eta(X_t, \mu_{i,t}, \Sigma_{i,t}) \tag{1}$$

where K is the number of Gaussian distributions, $\omega_{i,t}$, $\mu_{i,t}$, $\Sigma_{i,t}$ are respectively the weight estimate, the mean value and the co-variance matrix of the ith Gaussian in the model at time t and η is the Gaussian probability density given by:

$$\eta(X_t, \mu, \Sigma) = 1/(2\pi)^{N/2} \mid \Sigma \mid^{1/2} \exp^{-1/2(X_t - \mu_t)^T \Sigma^{-1}(X_t - \mu_t)} \tag{2}$$

For computational reasons, the authors in [46] assumed that the Red-Green-Blue color components are independent and have the same variance $\sigma_{i,t}^2$.

Therefore, the covariance matrix could be written as follows:

$$\Sigma_{i,t} = \sigma_{i,t}^2 I \tag{3}$$

An on-line K-means approximation is employed where every new pixel value, X_t, is tested for match with the existing K Gaussian distributions. If the value of the pixel lies within 2.5 standard deviation of a distribution then it is said to be matched. If there is no match for all of the K distributions, the mean value of the least probable distribution is updated with the current value, its variance is initialized with a high value, and it is assigned a low prior weight [4]. The weights for K distributions are updated as follows:

$$\omega_{k,t} = (1 - \alpha) + \alpha(M_{k,t}) \tag{4}$$

where α is the learning rate and $M_{k,t} = 1$ for the matched model and $M_{k,t} = 0$ for the remaining models. The ratio $\omega_{i,t}/\sigma_{i,t}$ is a discriminating factor that separates the background from the foreground. After sorting the Gaussians by the value of $\omega_{i,t}/\sigma_{i,t}$, we choose the first B distributions as the background model, B is computed as follows:

$$B = argmin_b(\sum_{i=1}^{b} \omega_{i,t} > T) \tag{5}$$

where T is the minimum portion of the background model.

Gaussian mixture model (GMM) is a popular method for detecting moving object such as vehicle. In [38], the moving objects present in the foreground are detected using Gaussian Mixture Model and Blob Analysis.

In [3], the GMM was combined with a kalman filter based object tracking method for vehicle detection.

3.1.2   Gaussian Mixture Model and Blob Analysis

In this subsection, we explain the GMM process to perform foreground segmentation and vehicle detection through blob analysis. This approach substitutes the entire video processing by an initial segmentation of the moving objects from the first frames. A certain number of video frames is needed for the foreground detection in order to initialize the Gaussian mixture model. We used the first 50 frames to initialize 5 Gaussian modes in the mixture model. We set the value of Gaussian modes greater than 3 to model multiple background modes. GMM is initialized with the number of Gaussians, the minimum background ratio, the learning rate and the number of training frames. After the training, the detector starts to produce more reliable segmentation results. The foreground segmentation process is imperfect and often provides undesirable noise. This method employs morphological opening to eliminate the noise and to fill holes in the detected objects. Blob analysis object is employed then to get bounding boxes around each connected component. The object further filters the detected foreground by rejecting blobs having less than 1600 pixels. The remaining video frames are processed similarly.

3.2 Optical Flow

3.2.1 Optical Flow Algorithm

Optical flow approaches employ the flow vectors of moving objects over time in order to detect moving regions in an image [40,50]. In [52], the authors propose to combine optical flow and self-adaptive threshold segmentation in order to detect moving object. It is based on the hypothesis that intensity I of moving pixel is constant in successive frames. It is calculated by getting two images at time t and $t + \delta t$.

$$I(x,y,t) = I(x + \delta x, y + \delta y, t + \delta t) \tag{6}$$

Employing Taylor series, the above equation is extended to:

$$I(x+\delta x, y+\delta y, t+\delta t) = I(x,y,t) + dI/dx\delta x + dI/dy\delta y + dI/dt\delta t + H.O.T \tag{7}$$

Averting higher order terms $(H.O.T.)$, the equation is restricted to:

$$dI/dx\delta x + dI/dy\delta y + dI/dt\delta t = 0 \tag{8}$$

$$I(x+\delta x, y+\delta y, t+\delta t) = I(x,y,t) + dI/dx\delta x + dI/dy\delta y + dI/dt\delta t + H.O.T \tag{9}$$

$$dI/dx(\delta x/\delta t) + dI/dy(\delta y/\delta t) + dI/dt = 0 \tag{10}$$

$$dI/dxV_x + dI/dyV_y + dI/dt = 0 \tag{11}$$

$$I_xV_x + I_yV_y = -I_t \tag{12}$$

where Vx, Vy represents optical flow vectors and Ix, Iy represent derivatives of the image intensities at coordinate (x, y, t). The values Vx, Vy are employed to obtain the motion vector for the detected object using threshold method. Magnitude of motion vector is defined as:

$$Th = \sqrt{V_x^2 + V_y^2} \tag{13}$$

Threshold is applied on this Th value. Then, the moving object is detected using the morphological operations.

In the literature, various researches have used optical flow to detect and track vehicle. In [9] the authors detected moving vehicle using optical flow estimation on an edge image. Another approach is presented in [2], where the motion detection and tracking system is implemented based on optical flow estimation and blob analysis is used for object segmentation. In [35], the authors used Optical flow algorithm and background subtraction to detect and track the vehicle motion along the frames.

3.2.2 Optical Flow and Blob Analysis

After using optical flow computation to detect motion vectors, objects are extracted from the background by thresholding the vector magnitudes. To eliminate the speckle noise the filtering process is applied and finally blob analysis is used to recognize the vehicles to be tracked. Due to weather conditions, various operations like speckle, impulse and general external noises filtering are introduced. The filtering operation generally produces holes in the processed frames and in order to fill them and therefore reduce detection errors, morphological closing is performed. Moving objects are then detected and the blob analysis serves to cluster objects which cannot be cars based on blob sizes. Finally, bounding boxes around the vehicles are drawn.

3.3 Aggregate Channel Features

Currently, new training-based detectors particularly employing deep learning schemes, have been presented to identify objects in images. Various learning-based object detectors like Aggregate Channel Features (ACF) [5], Region-Based Convolutional Neural Network (RCNN) [19], FastRCNN [17], FasterRCNN [23], and You Only Look Once (YOLO) [36], have been used for object detection. Some of these detectors have been adapted for vehicle detection such as Faster-RCNN [15].

For an ACF detector, a channel makes reference to a certain component that represents pixel values in image. Using obtained channels, ACF produces different features. These features, called channel features, can be divided into two types: first-order and high-order channels. The first order channel features are selected from a particular channel by summing pixels and the second type is obtained by mixing two or more first-order channel features. Decision tree is then used for classification. In this comparative study we have used the ACF object detector for vehicle detection. It is trained by labeling the object of interest in the first frame which allows to detect this object in the next frames. The detector employs a pre-trained model to detect object in the space dimension and another trained classifier to associate the objects in the time dimension. Then a short-term tracker is employed to update the detector over time. The tracking process is divided into two tasks; detecting objects in frames and finding the object of interest among the objects of each frame.

In this paper, the object of interest tracking is performed using a tracking-by-detection approach where the same object is identified in consecutive frames of the video. The object detector executes the first step and a time series analyzer is then applied for tracking. A detector is trained with the positive and negative data produced from the first frame and it is then applied for the following frames in the video, the detector is re-trained with the currently detected objects in the video part. In [30], a comparative study of different tracking-by-detection methods on public datasets is presented.

4   Experimentation

Our main objective in this paper is to investigate the performances of three vehicle detection methods, namely GMM and blob analysis, optical flow combined with blob analysis, ACF object detector. We evaluate these methods under different weather and traffic conditions.

In the following, we first present our own dataset, the used metrics for the evaluation before exposing the obtained results.

4.1   Dataset

In order to evaluate the presented methods for vehicle detection, we use a dataset containing 180 video sequences from two cameras placed on the bridge of Bizerte. These videos include different scenes filmed during daylight, in different dates and under different weather conditions (sunny, rainy).

To evaluate our ACF vehicle detector we used 84 video sequences for training and 96 video sequences for testing.

Table 1 describes the dataset characteristics for the two cameras.

Table 1. The dataset characteristics

	Camera 1	Camera 2
Number of video sequence (sunny, rainy)	45	45
Frame rate	15	12
Number of images for each video sequence	225	195
Resolution	960*1080	960*1080

Figures 1 and 2 show frames samples of the traffic surveillance video from camera 1 and camera 2.

Before applying the different methods for vehicle detection, we apply a thresholding of pixel intensities variance over the video in order to perform road extraction.

Figures 3 and 4 show the results of the road extraction for camera 1 and camera 2.

4.2   Evaluation Metrics

The considered methods are evaluated using the standard performance metrics, namely precision, recall and accuracy. Recall metric measures how many vehicles are correctly detected, while precision refers to the detection accuracy rate in comparison to ground truth. We use the accuracy metric to represent the ratio of the correctly labelled vehicles to the whole pool of vehicles. These measures are computed as follows:

Fig. 1. Frame samples captured by camera 1 in different weather conditions (a) rainy (b) sunny

Fig. 2. Frame samples captured by camera 2 in different weather conditions (a) rainy (b) sunny

$$Recall = TP/TP + FN \tag{14}$$

$$Precision = TP/TP + FP \tag{15}$$

$$Accuracy = TP + TN/TP + FP + TN + FN \tag{16}$$

where TP (true positives) means the number of true vehicles which are correctly extracted, FP (False Positives) represents the number of falsely detected vehicles,

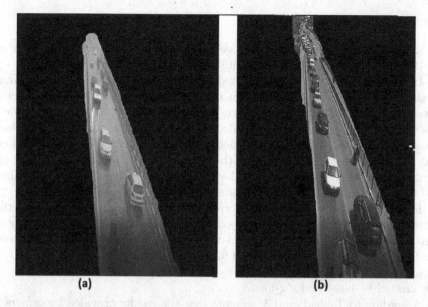

Fig. 3. Road extraction for camera 1 in different weather conditions (a) rainy (b) sunny

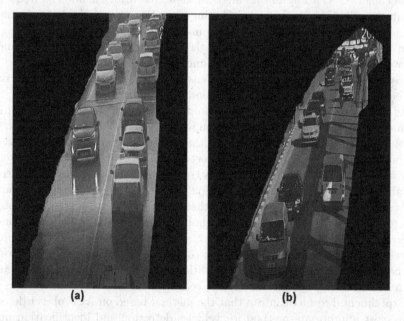

Fig. 4. Road extraction for camera 2 in different weather conditions (a) rainy (b) sunny

FN (False Negatives) is the number of missing vehicles and TN (True Negatives) is the number of non-vehicle.

4.3   Results and Discussion

In the first step of our experiment, we compare the three methods without considering the weather or traffic conditions.

In Table 2, we present a comparison of the results given by the different methods for camera 1. The detection method based on ACF Object Detector outperforms the other methods. It gives percentages over 90% for the three metrics which are considered as a good detection indices. The optical flow method allows to have the second best recall percentage, but it gives the lowest precision and accuracy percentages than the other methods. This could be explained by the fact that this method allows to have a high number of false positive pixel and therefore a lower precision and accuracy values.

From the results provided by camera 2 presented in Table 3, we note that the detection method based on ACF Object Detector has the better results for the three metrics, which proves the effectiveness of this approach. The GMM has the following results: it has a recall of 62%, a precision of 80% and it gives a low accuracy of 57%. The optical flow gives the lowest precision percentage because it's affected by noise and shadow.

According to Tables 2 and 3, we note that the results provided by camera 1 for the various approaches are better than those obtained from camera 2. Due to the camera 2 location and its angle of view, the bridge shadow is frequently present on the video sequences, affecting therefore the methods performance especially optical flow and GMM based methods.

In what follows, we consider jointly the video sequences from the 2 cameras and we compute the recall, precision and accuracy metrics according to the two commonly existing weather conditions in video sequences: sunny and rainy weather (Table 4) and to three traffic conditions (Table 5).

As we can see from Table 4, the performances of the GMM and Optical flow methods decline in rainy days, the reason may be due to luminosity problem and the blur caused by fog. We can deduce that these two methods are sensitive to weather conditions, while the ACF detector maintains its performance even in rainy days. In fact, the ACF detector is trained using a long video sequence, so it is able to detect with a higher precision the different vehicles on the road.

According to Table 5, we can see that the method based on ACF object detector outperforms also the other methods in the different traffic conditions. It has a recall of 100 % for the light traffic condition and it is able to detect vehicles, under severe occlusions in heavy traffic conditions, by reaching 91%. However, for the other methods, the traffic conditions deeply affect their performances which decrease with the increase of the vehicles number.

Experimental results confirm that the method based on ACF object detector is the most appropriate method for vehicles detection and identification under different weather conditions and illumination changes. This method is able to detect only the vehicles, however, its performances tightly depend on the training data size. In the other side, optical flow based method can successfully detect

Table 2. Comparison of various methods of vehicle detection for camera 1

Method detection	Recall %	Precision %	Accuracy %
GMM	77	84	75
Optical flow	97	75	73
ACF object detector	98	93	95

Table 3. Comparison of various methods of vehicle detection for camera2

Method detection	Recall %	Precision %	Accuracy %
GMM	62	80	57
Optical flow	90	70	67
ACF object detector	92	98	92

Table 4. Comparison of the different methods according to weather condition variation

Method	Weather condition					
	Sunny			Rainy		
	Recall %	Precision %	Accuracy %	Recall %	Precision %	Accuracy %
GMM	67	83	67	63	82	65
Optical flow	94	72	72	92	70	67
ACF object detector	95	94	92	95	97	94

Table 5. Comparison of the different methods according to traffic condition variation

Method/traffic condition	Light			Medium			Heavy		
	Recall %	Precision %	Accuracy %	Recall %	Precision %	Accuracy %	Recall %	Precision %	Accuracy %
GMM	81	84	80	68	85	65	59	77	53
Optical flow	94	65	65	94	74	73	92	75	57
ACF object detector	100	92	95	94	100	95	91	95	89

even occluded vehicles. But it is deeply affected by noise and shadow as other moving objects like persons and motorcycles can be also detected. The method using GMM is a fast and accurate detection technique in normal conditions. Nevertheless , this method is very sensitive to weather conditions and illumination changes.

In Table 6 pros and cons of various methods have been discussed.

Table 6. Pros and Cons of various methods of vehicle detection

Method	Pros	Cons
GMM	Fast technique	Very sensitive to weather conditions changes
	Precision of detection is good	Failure in the detection if the brightness is high
	Occlusion handling	
Optical flow	Accuracy of detection is good	Affected by noise and shadow
	Occlusion handle	Detect other moving objects like person and motorcycle
ACF object detector	Recall is good	complex
	Detect only the vehicles	Need many training data

5   Conclusion

In this paper, three approaches for vehicle detection have been studied namely GMM and blob analysis, optical flow combined with blob analysis, ACF object detector. The experimental results show that the vehicle detection method based on ACF object detector outperforms the other methods regardless the weather or traffic conditions due to its robustness to external factors when it is well trained. Sensitivity to weather or traffic conditions and occlusion handling are good criteria for vehicles detection method selection. However, the time required for feature extraction is also an important criterion for detector selection especially for real time applications. Thus, we have to select the vehicle detection method providing the best trade off between detection performances and system runtime.

Acknowledgment. This work was financially supported by the PHC Utique program of the French Ministry of Foreign Affairs and Ministry of higher education and research and the Tunisian Ministry of higher education and scientific research in the CMCU project number 17G1417.

References

1. Ahmed, W., Arafat, S.Y., Gul, N.: A systematic review on vehicle identification and classification techniques. In: 2018 IEEE 21st International Multi-Topic Conference (INMIC), pp. 1–6. IEEE (2018)
2. Aslani, S., Mahdavi-Nasab, H.: Optical flow based moving object detection and tracking for traffic surveillance. Int. J. Electr. Comput. Energ. Electron. Commun. Eng. **7**(9), 1252–1256 (2013)
3. Bakti, R.Y., Areni, I.S., Prayogi, A.A., et al.: Vehicle detection and tracking using Gaussian Mixture Model and Kalman Filter. In: 2016 International Conference on Computational Intelligence and Cybernetics, pp. 115–119. IEEE (2016)

4. Bouwmans, T., El Baf, F., Vachon, B.: Background modeling using mixture of Gaussians for foreground detection-a survey. Recent Pat. Comput. Sci. **1**(3), 219–237 (2008)
5. Byeon, Y.H., Kwak, K.C.: A performance comparison of pedestrian detection using faster RCNN and ACF. In: 2017 6th IIAI International Congress on Advanced Applied Informatics (IIAI-AAI), pp. 858–863. IEEE (2017)
6. Chang, W.C., Cho, C.W.: Online boosting for vehicle detection. IEEE Trans. Syst. Man Cybern. Part B (Cybern.) **40**(3), 892–902 (2009)
7. Charouh, Z., Ghogho, M., Guennoun, Z.: Improved background subtraction-based moving vehicle detection by optimizing morphological operations using machine learning. In: 2019 IEEE International Symposium on INnovations in Intelligent SysTems and Applications (INISTA), pp. 1–6. IEEE (2019)
8. Chen, D., Jin, G., Lu, L., Tan, L., Wei, W.: Infrared image vehicle detection based on Haar-like feature. In: 2018 IEEE 3rd Advanced Information Technology, Electronic and Automation Control Conference (IAEAC), pp. 662–667. IEEE (2018)
9. Chen, Y., Wu, Q.: Moving vehicle detection based on optical flow estimation of edge. In: 2015 11th International Conference on Natural Computation (ICNC), pp. 754–758. IEEE (2015)
10. Cheng, H.Y.: Highway traffic flow estimation for surveillance scenes damaged by rain. IEEE Intell. Syst. **33**(1), 64–77 (2018)
11. Cherkaoui, B., Beni-Hssane, A., El Fissaoui, M., Erritali, M.: Road traffic congestion detection in VANET networks. Procedia Comput. Sci. **151**, 1158–1163 (2019)
12. Choudhury, S., Chattopadhyay, S.P., Hazra, T.K.: Vehicle detection and counting using Haar feature-based classifier. In: 2017 8th Annual Industrial Automation and Electromechanical Engineering Conference (IEMECON), pp. 106–109. IEEE (2017)
13. Dalal, N., Triggs, B.: Histograms of oriented gradients for human detection. In: CVPR, vol. 1, pp. 886–893. IEEE Computer Society (2005)
14. Elkerdawi, S.M., Sayed, R., ElHelw, M.: Real-time vehicle detection and tracking using Haar-like features and compressive tracking. In: Armada, M.A., Sanfeliu, A., Ferre, M. (eds.) ROBOT2013: First Iberian Robotics Conference. AISC, vol. 252, pp. 381–390. Springer, Cham (2014). https://doi.org/10.1007/978-3-319-03413-3_27
15. Fan, Q., Brown, L., Smith, J.: A closer look at faster R-CNN for vehicle detection. In: 2016 IEEE Intelligent Vehicles Symposium (IV), pp. 124–129. IEEE (2016)
16. Gazzah, S., Mhalla, A., Amara, N.E.B.: Vehicle detection on a video traffic scene: review and new perspectives. In: 2016 7th International Conference on Sciences of Electronics, Technologies of Information and Telecommunications (SETIT), pp. 448–454. IEEE (2016)
17. Girshick, R.: Fast R-CNN. In: Proceedings of the IEEE International Conference on Computer Vision, pp. 1440–1448 (2015)
18. Girshick, R., Donahue, J., Darrell, T., Malik, J.: Rich feature hierarchies for accurate object detection and semantic segmentation. In: Proceedings of the IEEE Conference on Computer Vision and Pattern Recognition, pp. 580–587 (2014)
19. Girshick, R., Donahue, J., Darrell, T., Malik, J.: Region-based convolutional networks for accurate object detection and segmentation. IEEE Trans. Pattern Anal. Mach. Intell. **38**(1), 142–158 (2015)
20. Hsu, S.C., Huang, C.L., Chuang, C.H.: Vehicle detection using simplified fast R-CNN. In: 2018 International Workshop on Advanced Image Technology (IWAIT), pp. 1–3. IEEE (2018)

21. Jain, N.K., Saini, R.K., Mittal, P.: A review on traffic monitoring system techniques. In: Ray, K., Sharma, T.K., Rawat, S., Saini, R.K., Bandyopadhyay, A. (eds.) Soft Computing: Theories and Applications. AISC, vol. 742, pp. 569–577. Springer, Singapore (2019). https://doi.org/10.1007/978-981-13-0589-4_53

22. Kul, S., Eken, S., Sayar, A.: A concise review on vehicle detection and classification. In: 2017 International Conference on Engineering and Technology (ICET), pp. 1–4. IEEE (2017)

23. Liu, B., Zhao, W., Sun, Q.: Study of object detection based on faster R-CNN. In: 2017 Chinese Automation Congress (CAC), pp. 6233–6236. IEEE (2017)

24. Liu, Y., Tian, B., Chen, S., Zhu, F., Wang, K.: A survey of vision-based vehicle detection and tracking techniques in ITS. In: Proceedings of 2013 IEEE International Conference on Vehicular Electronics and Safety, pp. 72–77. IEEE (2013)

25. Marcomini, L., Cunha, A.: A comparison between background modelling methods for vehicle segmentation in highway traffic videos. arXiv preprint arXiv:1810.02835 (2018)

26. Martin, R., Bruce, G.: Monitoring traffic flow. US Patent App. 10/431,077, 1 Oct 2019

27. Misman, N., Awang, S.: Camera-based vehicle recognition methods and techniques: systematic literature review. Adv. Sci. Lett. 24(10), 7623–7629 (2018)

28. Mo, G., Zhang, Y., Zhang, S., Zhou, X., Yan, J.: A method of vehicle detection based on sift features and boosting classifier. J. Converg. Inf. Technol. 7(12), 328–334 (2012)

29. Mohamed, A., Issam, A., Mohamed, B., Abdellatif, B.: Real-time detection of vehicles using the Haar-like features and artificial neuron networks. Procedia Comput. Sci. 73, 24–31 (2015)

30. Moussy, E., Mekonnen, A.A., Marion, G., Lerasle, F.: A comparative view on exemplar 'tracking-by-detection' approaches. In: 2015 12th IEEE International Conference on Advanced Video and Signal Based Surveillance (AVSS), pp. 1–6. IEEE (2015)

31. Mu, K., Hui, F., Zhao, X.: Multiple vehicle detection and tracking in highway traffic surveillance video based on sift feature matching. J. Inf. Process. Syst. 12(2), 183–195 (2016)

32. Mukhtar, A., Xia, L., Tang, T.B.: Vehicle detection techniques for collision avoidance systems: a review. IEEE Trans. Intell. Transp. Syst. 16(5), 2318–2338 (2015)

33. Nguyen, M.Q., Pham, T.T.X., Phan, T.T.H.: Traffic congestion. Eur. J. Eng. Res. Sci. 4(9), 112–116 (2019)

34. Oheka, O., Tu, C.: Real-time multiple vehicle detection using a rear camera mounted on a vehicle. In: 2018 International Conference on Intelligent and Innovative Computing Applications (ICONIC), pp. 1–5. IEEE (2018)

35. Paygude, S., Vibha, V., Manisha, C.: Vehicle detection and tracking using the opticalflow and background subtraction. In: Proceedings of International Conference on Advances in Computer Science and Application (2013)

36. Redmon, J., Divvala, S., Girshick, R., Farhadi, A.: You only look once: unified, real-time object detection. In: Proceedings of the IEEE Conference on Computer Vision and Pattern Recognition, pp. 779–788 (2016)

37. Ren, S., He, K., Girshick, R., Sun, J.: Faster R-CNN: towards real-time object detection with region proposal networks. In: Advances in Neural Information Processing Systems, pp. 91–99 (2015)

38. Santosh, D.H.H., Venkatesh, P., Poornesh, P., Rao, L.N., Kumar, N.A.: Tracking multiple moving objects using Gaussian Mixture Model. Int. J. Soft Comput. Eng. (IJSCE) 3(2), 114–119 (2013)

39. Saund, E.: System and method for visual motion based object segmentation and tracking. US Patent 9,025,825, 5 May 2015
40. Sharma, V., Nain, N., Badal, T.: A survey on moving object detection methods in video surveillance. Int. Bull. Math. Res. **2**(1), 208–218 (2015)
41. Shehata, M., Abo-Al-Ez, R., Zaghlool, F., Abou-Kreisha, M.T.: Vehicles detection based on background modeling. arXiv preprint arXiv:1901.04077 (2019)
42. Shobha, B., Deepu, R.: A review on video based vehicle detection, recognition and tracking. In: 2018 3rd International Conference on Computational Systems and Information Technology for Sustainable Solutions (CSITSS), pp. 183–186. IEEE (2018)
43. Sivaraman, S., Trivedi, M.M.: A review of recent developments in vision-based vehicle detection. In: 2013 IEEE Intelligent Vehicles Symposium (IV), pp. 310–315. IEEE (2013)
44. Sivaraman, S., Trivedi, M.M.: Looking at vehicles on the road: a survey of vision-based vehicle detection, tracking, and behavior analysis. IEEE Trans. Intell. Transp. Syst. **14**(4), 1773–1795 (2013)
45. Soleh, M., Jati, G., Hilman, M.H.: Multi object detection and tracking using optical flow density-hungarian kalman filter (ofd-Hkf) algorithm for vehicle counting. Jurnal Ilmu Komputer dan Informasi **11**(1), 17–26 (2018)
46. Stauffer, C., Grimson, W.E.L.: Adaptive background mixture models for real-time tracking. In: IEEE Computer Society Conference on Computer Vision and Pattern Recognition, 1999, vol. 2. IEEE (1999)
47. Sun, Z., Bebis, G., Miller, R.: On-road vehicle detection: a review. IEEE Trans. Pattern Anal. Mach. Intell. **28**(5), 694–711 (2006)
48. Tsai, L.W., Hsieh, J.W., Fan, K.C.: Vehicle detection using normalized color and edge map. IEEE Trans. Image Process. **16**(3), 850–864 (2007)
49. Uijlings, J.R., Van De Sande, K.E., Gevers, T., Smeulders, A.W.: Selective search for object recognition. Int. J. Comput. Vis. **104**(2), 154–171 (2013)
50. Viswanath, A., Behera, R.K., Senthamilarasu, V., Kutty, K.: Background modelling from a moving camera. Procedia Comput. Sci. **58**, 289–296 (2015)
51. Wang, G., Xiao, D., Gu, J.: Review on vehicle detection based on video for traffic surveillance. In: 2008 IEEE International Conference on Automation and Logistics, pp. 2961–2966. IEEE (2008)
52. Wei, S.G., Yang, L., Chen, Z., Liu, Z.F.: Motion detection based on optical flow and self-adaptive threshold segmentation. Procedia Eng. **15**, 3471–3476 (2011)
53. Wei, Y., Tian, Q., Guo, J., Huang, W., Cao, J.: Multi-vehicle detection algorithm through combining Harr and HOG features. Math. Comput. Simul. **155**, 130–145 (2019)
54. Wu, L.-T., Tran, V.L., Lin, H.-Y.: Real-time overtaking vehicle detection based on optical flow and convolutional neural network. In: Donnellan, B., Klein, C., Helfert, M., Gusikhin, O. (eds.) SMARTGREENS/VEHITS -2018. CCIS, vol. 992, pp. 227–243. Springer, Cham (2019). https://doi.org/10.1007/978-3-030-26633-2_11
55. Zhou, J., Duan, J., Yu, H.: Machine-vision based preceding vehicle detection algorithm: a review. In: Proceedings of the 10th World Congress on Intelligent Control and Automation, pp. 4617–4622. IEEE (2012)
56. Zhuang, X., Kang, W., Wu, Q.: Real-time vehicle detection with foreground-based cascade classifier. IET Image Proc. **10**(4), 289–296 (2016)

Distributed Computing for Networking and Communication

Energy Efficient Handshake Algorithm for Wireless Sensor Networks

Emna Taktak[1]([✉])(iD), Mohamed Tounsi[1,3](iD), Mohamed Mosbah[2](iD),
and Ahmed Hadj Kacem[1](iD)

[1] ReDCAD Laboratory, University of Sfax, Sfax, Tunisia
`emna.taktak@redcad.org`, {`mohamed.tounsi,ahmed.hadjkacem`}`@fsegs.rnu.tn`
[2] Univ. Bordeaux, CNRS, Bordeaux INP, LaBRI, UMR 5800, 33400 Talence, France
`mohamed.mosbah@u-bordeaux.fr`
[3] Umm Al-Qura University, Mecca, Saudi Arabia

Abstract. A Wireless Sensor Network (WSN) is composed of sensors
that communicate together in a distributed way to supervise the environment. The energy consumption is an important performance measure for
a WSN that spurs the development of energy-efficient distributed algorithms for WSNs. In this field, we focus on a specific type of distributed
algorithms called handshake. A handshake algorithm allows making two
sensors communicate safely by ensuring that they communicate together
in an exclusive mode. In this paper, we propose a new energy-efficient
WSN Handshake algorithm (WSN-HS). We present an evaluation of our
algorithm compared to another similar one. The simulation results show
that when using our WSN-HS, we can save the energy of the sensors and
minimise the total number of exchanged messages. Alongside with its
energy efficiency, our algorithm is fault-tolerant. Hence, we make the disappearance of some sensors caused by their energy depletion not blocking
for other sensors.

Keywords: Handshake algorithm · Wireless Sensor Network · Energy
efficiency · Fault tolerance

1 Introduction

A Wireless Sensor Network (WSN) consists of sensors communicating together
in a distributed manner to supervise the environment. Distributed algorithms
are employed in WSNs because they ensure the scalability of these networks,
i.e., allow to manage a large number of sensors. For example, authors in [2] propose a new distributed algorithm for leader election in WSN because it ensures
good performance, scalability, and reliability compared to a centralised algorithm. Also, they affirm that thanks to distributed algorithms we have sensors
that work in parallel. Consequently, if a sensor crashes, the network should give a
correct execution result. Moreover, authors in [14] propose a distributed scheduling algorithm of the clustering task in a WSN. This algorithm is scalable and

© Springer Nature Switzerland AG 2020
I. Jemili and M. Mosbah (Eds.): DiCES-N 2019, CCIS 1130, pp. 57–76, 2020.
https://doi.org/10.1007/978-3-030-40131-3_4

energy-efficient. As an example of distributed algorithms for WSNs, we focus on the handshake algorithms. A handshake is a fact that communication is realised only if two sensors wait for it. The handshake algorithm is like a local process that realises a temporary and exclusive synchronisation between two neighbours in an asynchronous automatic and random way. The handshake algorithm relies on the Local Computation on Edges model (LCE) [10] allowing sensors to communicate in pairs. Thanks to the LCE model, communications can be realised in parallel i.e., at the same time with no risk of collision and that is because the sensors exchange their information only if they are synchronised [1]. Once the pairs are synchronised (there is a handshake), they exchange their information and then the distributed algorithm can be executed.

Unfortunately, most of the used handshake algorithms [8,9,12] do an arbitrary choice of the communicating nodes without considering the remaining energy of the sensors. Although, the energy consumption is a very important performance measure for a WSN, especially for a WSN where sensors are supplied by batteries. Therefore, a handshake algorithm should take into consideration the energy level of sensors when choosing the communicating pairs to save the energy of sensors and maximise their lifetime. Besides, WSNs are widely used for critical systems (military, health-care, etc.), consequently, we should ensure that the distributed algorithms continue to be executed when the energy of some sensors is depleted.

To solve the problems listed above, in this paper, we propose a new handshake algorithm that takes into consideration the energy consumption of sensors. Our proposed algorithm is not only energy-efficient but also fault-tolerant to sensors disappearance. Our new algorithm is dubbed WSN-HS for Wireless Sensor Network Handshake algorithm.

We mention that in [7], authors propose a solution that makes any algorithm designed with the population protocols [4] tolerant to a certain type of sensors failure. Therefore, authors create a general-purpose conversion that transforms an algorithm A to another fault-tolerant algorithm B. This is different from our work because we do not change any of the existing distributed algorithms. We treat the fault tolerance aspect at the synchronisation level independently from the executed distributed algorithm which makes our solution more simple and easy to use. Moreover, we consider the energy consumption of sensors alongside the fault tolerance problem which is not the case for the proposed solution in [7].

To evaluate the performance of our WSN-HS algorithm, we make a simulation using two distributed algorithms: leader election in tree topology and dead animals algorithm. These algorithms are simulated firstly with a similar handshake algorithm [9] and secondly with our WSN-HS. We choose these two algorithms because they represent a class of algorithms applied for WSNs. Many distributed algorithms for WSN are based on leader election (clustering, etc.), also, many others are designed to carter problems similar to the problem dressed by the dead animals algorithm. Hence, the simulation emphasises that our WSN-HS minimises the energy consumption of the sensors with a low battery level to keep them alive as long as possible. Furthermore, it reduces the energy consumption of the WSN in general by reducing the number of needed messages to establish synchronisations in the network.

The remainder of the paper is organised as follows: Sect. 2 details the related work. Section 3 defines some basic concepts. Section 4 details our WSN-HS. Section 5 explains the functioning of the simulated distributed algorithms. Section 6 presents the gathered simulation results. The last Section concludes the paper and highlights some future work.

2   Related Work

In [12], authors present a representative work dealing with the handshake algorithms. Their proposed algorithm is called Synchronous Non-Fault-Tolerant Handshake (SNH). This algorithm is synchronous and needs just one bit to encode messages. It is laid out in the following as Algorithm 1 . The weak point of this algorithm is the large number of sent messages sent in the network. Also, it is not fault-tolerant. Our algorithm is different from this algorithm since it is asynchronous.

Algorithm 1. SNH [9]

---

1 Each node p repeats these actions:
2 node p chooses one of its neighbours $c(p)$ randomly;
3 node p sends 1 to $c(p)$;
4 node p sends 0 to its neighbours except $c(p)$;
5 node p receives the messages of its neighbours;
6 (*p and $c(p)$ do a handshake when p receives 1 from $c(p)$.*)

As an asynchronous handshake algorithm, authors in [9] present a new randomised handshake algorithm for pairwise asynchronous communications in a distributed system. This algorithm ameliorates the algorithm proposed in [12] by making it fault-tolerant. This Asynchronous Fault-Tolerant Handshake algorithm (ATH) is more interesting than the existing algorithms [6] because it is asynchronous. If a graph contains some faulty nodes, then they will affect only their direct neighbours. This is called a contaminated area. Thus, synchronisations may exist for nodes located out of this zone. The authors proved that the ATH algorithm ensures a good efficiency expressed as a ratio between the synchronisation attempts and the succeeded synchronisations. This ATH algorithm is presented in the following: As expressed by Algorithm 2 , each sensor node p picks one of its neighbours randomly c(p) to have a handshake. As a result of this choice, the node p sends a message that contains 1 to c(p). After that, p waits to receive a message from c(p). Thereby, each node p has three different possibilities.

Algorithm 2. ATH algorithm [9]

---

1 Each node p does these actions:
2 p chooses one of its neighbours $c(p)$ randomly;
3 p sends 1 to $c(p)$;
4 p receives a message m from a neighbour w;
5 **if** $w=c(p)$ *and* $m = 1$ **then**
6   do a computation; //p *and* $c(p)$ *are doing a handshake*
7   return to step 2;
8 **else**
9   **if** $w = c(p)$ *and* $m = 0$ **then**
10   return to step 2 ; // $c(p)$ *has chosen a node different from* p
11   **else**
12   p sends 0 to w ; // *in that case,* $m = 1$
13   return to step 4;

- First, the handshake is realised between p and c(p) if p receives 1 from c(p). In this case, p and c(p) will be doing a computation step of the distributed algorithm that needs synchronisation to be made before its execution. After that p re-executes the ATH algorithm.
- Second, the handshake is not possible if p receives 0 from c(p). In this case, c(p) picked another neighbour different from p. After that p re-executes the algorithm.
- Third, if p has not received a response from c(p), it stays on waiting for the response. At this same, if p received 1 from w ≠ c(p), then p sends 0 to w. Consequently, in this phase, p can not send any 1-messages.

It is clear from Algorithm 2 that the reception of messages is not blocking. A node p in the network can respond to its neighbours with messages containing 0 even before receiving a response from its chosen neighbour c(p). Moreover, when a node is faulty, it can not send messages to its neighbours anymore.

Unfortunately, the ATH algorithm is not suitable for WSNs. Although it is fault-tolerant, it is not fault-tolerant of sensors' disappearance. In a WSN, sensors frequently disappear from the network because of their energy depletion. Moreover, the ATH is not energy efficient, many messages are needed to establish synchronisations between two sensors.

3 Basic Concepts

Our handshake algorithm is proposed for distributed algorithms that need synchronisations to be made between sensors before their execution. These algorithms must respect the Local Computations on Edges model (LCE). Hence, in the first part of this section, we recall the definition of the LCE model. The second part is dedicated to present a computations model that adapts the LCE model to the context of WSNs.

3.1   Local Computations on Edges Model (LCE)

The local computations model is based on the Graph Relabelling System [10] (GRS). With this model, we represent a network as a graph containing nodes that represent processors (sensors) and edges representing the bidirectional links between processors. At every time, each node and each edge is in some particular state, and this state will be encoded by a label. According to its state and the state of its neighbours, each node may decide to realise an elementary computation step. After this step, the state of this node, of its neighbours and the corresponding edges may have changed according to some specific computation rules called relabelling step. For such systems, the distributed aspect comes from the fact that several relabelling steps can be performed simultaneously on far enough (non-overlapping) sub-graphs.

The Local computations on edges model (LCE) is a special type of the local computations model. LCE is graph relabelling relations such that each relabelling step depends on and modifies only the labels of two adjacent nodes and the edge linking them. A relabelling step consists of (1) choosing, in a non-deterministic way, an edge on which a rule can be applied, and (2) modifying the labels of this edge with respect to the rule.

3.2   Local Computations Model for WSN

GRSs have been introduced as a suitable model for expressing and studying distributed algorithms on a network of communicating processors [13]. However, they do not capture the WSN particularity. For this reason, the model proposed in [15] adapts the GRS used in the LCE model for modelling the distributed algorithms used in a WSN. This model allows proving the correctness of the modelled algorithms as shown in [16].

In fact, in a GRS, a state of a node/edge is encoded through several labels attached to it. This state is updated by a set of relabelling rules. Though, in [15], the state of a node is changed in response to two types of events:

- **Internal events** result from a capture made by a sensor, i.e, result from changes in the physical environment of a node. They are presented as internal relabelling rules.
- **External events** result from the communications made between sensors. The external events are presented as external relabelling rules.

In fact, with this model, a GRS is a quintuple $S = \{L_n, L_e, R_e, R_i, I\}$ with:

- L_n represents the alphabet for nodes labelling and L_e the alphabet for edges labelling. L_n is decomposed into two sets L_{n-ex} and L_{n-in}. The subset L_{n-in} represents the internal labels of a node (modified only by internal relabelling rules). Whereas L_{n-ex} represents the external labels of a node (modified by both internal and external relabelling rules).
- R_e is the set of external relabelling rules and R_i the set of internal relabelling rules.

– A function I which associates to the graph a set I_G of initial states.

In order to choose, in a non-deterministic way, an edge on which a rule can be applied, this model uses the handshake algorithms.

4 A New WSN Handshake Algorithm (WSN-HS)

In this paper, we propose a new WSN-HS algorithm. Our new algorithm is energy-efficient and fault-tolerant to sensors' disappearance. We address the issue of fault tolerance because it has immense practical importance in real sensor networks. When a sensor dies, say from an exhausted battery, many of the algorithms designed with the population protocols [4] for example would not survive [3], especially those based on leader election. Although, WSN algorithms are widely used in critical systems where non-fault-tolerant algorithms should not exist. Thus, our WSN-HS algorithm allows continuing the execution of the distributed algorithms even when a sensor dies. In fact, sensors will be informed when a neighbour sensor is dead.

Furthermore, the energy consumption is an important performance measure for a WSN. Although, it has not yet been considered by the existing models. Therefore in our new proposed algorithm, we encourage the appropriate use of sensors' energy. In addition, we reduce the global energy consumption in a WSN comparing to the ATH algorithm in [9] presented as Algorithm 2.

Our WSN-HS algorithm is presented as Algorithm 3 . In our new algorithm Algorithm 3 , we take into consideration the internal and external events introduced by the model in [15] presented in the previous section. There is no indication these events should be executed in which priority. For this reason, lines 3 and 4 of Algorithm 3 specify that the internal calculation (capture) should be executed first. Thus, before any handshake with a sensor (b), a sensor (a) should always checks if there is a new captured value. If it is the case, this concerned sensor updates its information/state as exemplified in Fig. 1. The motivation of this added priority is that a new captured value can influence the calculation made by the sensor after the synchronisation/handshake. For example, a new captured value can change a state of a sensor and as consequence can change the relabelling rule that will be executed after a handshake. In our new algorithm, after executing the internal events, a sensor always checks if it has enough energy

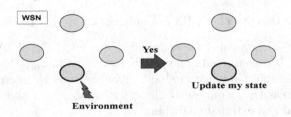

Fig. 1. Internal event

Algorithm 3. Our WSN-HS algorithm

---

1 Each node p does the following actions:
2 $waitingList \leftarrow null$;
3 if $\exists (internalCalculation)$ then
4   do $internalCalculation$

5 if $residualEnergy > threshold$ then
6   if $waitingList = null$ then
7   p chooses randomly one of its NeighbourList: $c(p)$;
8   p sends 1 to $c(p)$;
9   p receives a message m from a neighbour w;
10   else
11   p sends 1 to the first element in $waitingList$: $firstOne$;
12   p sends 0 to all other nodes in $waitingList$;
13        $waitingList \leftarrow null$; $m \leftarrow 1$; $c(p) \leftarrow firstOne$; $w \leftarrow firstOne$;
         $firstOne \leftarrow null$;
14   if $w = c(p)$ and $m = 1$ then
15   executeAlgo(); //p and $c(p)$ having a handshake and doing a computation step
16   return to line 3;
17   if $w = c(p)$ and $m = 0$ then
18   return to line 3 ; //$c(p)$ has chosen a node different from p
19   if $w \neq c(p)$ and $m = 1$ then
20   p sends 0 to w ;
21   return to line 5;
22   if $w = c(p)$ and $m = -1$ then
23   p delete w from the NeighbourList;
24   return to line 3;

25 else
26   if $residualEnergy < threshold$ then
27   if $waitingList = null$ then
28   p receives a message m from a neighbour w;
29   else
30           $firstOne \leftarrow pop(waitingList)$;
31           $w \leftarrow firstOne$;
32           $m \leftarrow 1$;
33   if $m = 1$ and $residualEnergy > opCost(w)$ then
34           $c(p) \leftarrow w$;
35   if $firstOne \neq null$ then
36   p sends 0 to all other nodes in $waitingList$;
37              $waitingList \leftarrow null$;
38              $firstOne \leftarrow null$;
39   executeAlgo(); //p and $c(p)$ having a handshake and doing a computation step
40   return to line 3;
41   if $m = 1$ and $residualEnergy < opCost(w)$ then
42   p sends -1 to w ;
43   return to line 3;
44   if $m = -1$ then
45   p delete w from the NeighbourList ;
46   return to line 3;

---

to send synchronisation demands. If it has enough energy, i.e, its residual energy is greater than a defined threshold (for example 30% of its total energy level), then this sensor sends synchronisation demands (line 5 to line 24 of Algorithm 3) as presented in Fig. 2. In case a sensor does not have enough energy, it does not send synchronisation demands but only responds to the received demands (line 26 to line 46 of Algorithm 3) as presented in Fig. 3. Thus, we can reduce the number of sent messages for a sensor with a low energy level. Therefore, we keep it alive for a longer period to communicate with other sensors.

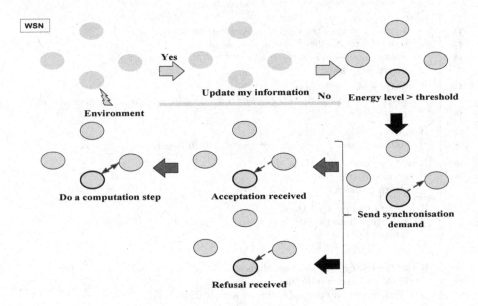

Fig. 2. External event with high energy level

Also, in Algorithm 3 , we introduce a new type of message comparing to Algorithm 2 . Hence, in Algorithm 2 , when a sensor (a) sends a message with a value equals to 1 to the sensor (b), it means that (a) accepts to synchronise with (b). When a sensor (a) sends a message with a value equals to 0 to the sensor (b), it means that (a) refuses to synchronise with (b). In Algorithm 3, a sensor (a) can also send a message with a value equals to -1 to (b) (line 41 to line 43 of Algorithm 3). This -1 message ("delete me" message in Fig. 3) means that (a) can not communicate with (b) and (b) should not send synchronisation demands to (a) anymore (line 22 to line 24 of Algorithm 3). This is because (a) has a low energy level that does not allow to communicate with (b) (the residual energy of (a) is less than the cost of a calculation with (b)). This cost is calculated based on different parameters like the distance linking the two communicating sensors for example.

When exchanging these types of messages between the sensors in the network, all these latter will be informed by the death of a sensor that runs out of energy.

Consequently, all distributed algorithms that will be used with this handshake algorithm will be fault-tolerant to sensors' disappearance.

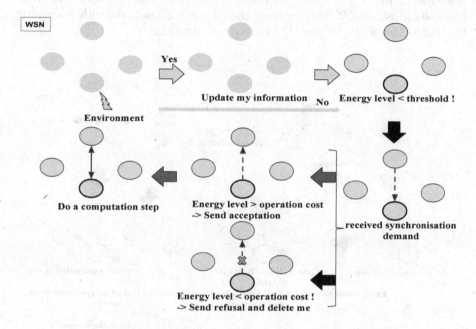

Fig. 3. External event with low energy level

As another new idea introduced by our algorithm, we mention that when two sensors (a) and (b) are synchronised, most of the time, they exchange their states through messages to be able to execute instructions of this distributed algorithm (line 2 to line 4 of Algorithm 4). Consequently, when a sensor (a) is executing instructions of the distributed algorithm with sensor (b), other sensors still can send synchronisation demands at this time (line 5 to line 7 of Algorithm 4). If this happens, (a) pushes the received synchronisation demands in the stack (waitingList) while it does computations with (b). After finishing computations with (b), sensor (a) will respond to the sensors waiting for handshakes. As mentioned in Algorithm 3 , if a sensor (a) has enough energy, it will accept the synchronisation demand of the first sensor (firstOne) in the list of waiting sensors (waitingList). Second, it will refuse all other synchronisation demands of other sensors (line 11 to line 13 of Algorithm 3). Instead of sending a synchronisation demand, sensor (a) will be automatically doing a handshake (with firstOne) and start to execute the distributed algorithm (line 14 to line 16 of Algorithm 3) as explained in Fig. 4. However, if (a) has not enough energy, it will take (and remove) the first sensor in the list of waiting sensors, if it can communicate with it (line 33 to line 40 of Algorithm 3), they will be doing a handshake together as stated in Fig. 4. In this case, (a) refuses the demands of other sensors in the waitingList. Otherwise, if (a) can not communicate with this first sensor, it will send a refusal and a −1 message to it. This −1 message informs the sensor that it should delete (a) from his neighbours list (line 41 to line 43 of Algorithm 3) as presented in Fig. 5. The sensor continues taking (and removing) elements from the waitingList until it finds a sensor that it can communicate with it or until the waitingList is empty (line 27 to line 32 of Algorithm 3).

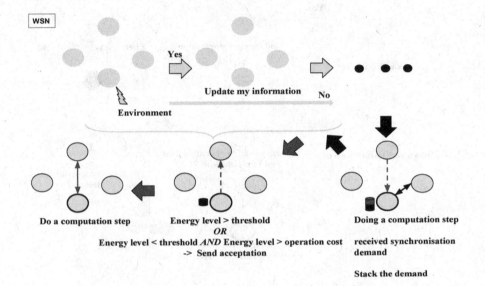

Fig. 4. Managing synchronisation demands of the waitingList: case of high energy level

---

Algorithm 4. executeAlgo()

---

1 instruction 1, 2, ...
2 **if** ∃*(informationExchange)* **then**
3   p sends its information to $c(p)$;
4   p receives a message *inf* from the neighbour *neig*;
5   **if** *neig* ≠ $c(p)$ *and inf* = 1 **then**
6   push *neig* in *waitingList*;
7   return to line 4;

8   **if** $w = c(p)$ **then**
9   instruction n, instruction n+1, ...

10 instruction m, instruction m+1, ... ;
11 return to Algorithm 1: line 3

The described mechanism allows to minimise the number of exchanged messages for all sensors in the network. Thus, when a sensor (a) saves a synchronisation demand and accepts it just after finishing its calculation, it avoids the procedure of sending a synchronisation demand, waiting for a response and maybe

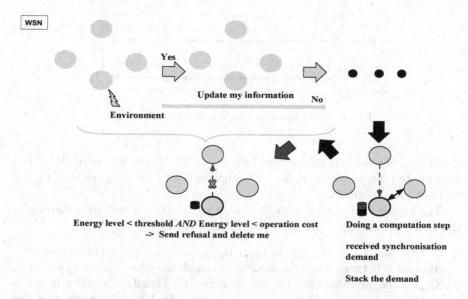

Fig. 5. Managing synchronisation demands of the waitingList: case of low energy level

receiving a refusal and re-sending another synchronisation demand, etc. We can wonder here why making other sensors waiting for a response from (a) while sensor (a) will accept only one sensor in the waiting list. In fact, if the sensor (a) responds to these other sensors before it finishes its calculation, they can re-send other synchronisation demands to the sensor (a) and (a) re-sends refusals, and this will be repeated in non-deterministic way. This procedure causes a big waste of messages. In addition, sensor (a) will waste much time responding to them each time.

5 Distributed Algorithms to Simulate

In this section, we expound the functioning of two distributed algorithms: the leader election and dead animals detection. These two algorithms are chosen as distributed algorithms to simulate with our WSN-HS presented as Algorithm 3 and the algorithm presented as Algorithm 2 .

5.1 Leader Election Algorithm

As a first simulated algorithm, we took an example of a classical algorithm used in the context of WSN: leader election in a tree topology. The leader election algorithm is represented in Fig. 6 as a set of relabelling rules specified with the local computations model in [15].

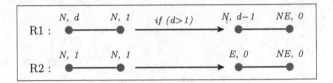

Fig. 6. Rules of leader election in a tree algorithm

The set of sensors is represented by a graph (G) having a tree topology. The sensors are represented as nodes (V) connected with links represented by the edges (E) in this graph.

The algorithm is coded with the following relabelling system according to the model presented in [15]: $S = \{L_n, L_e, R_e, R_i, I\}$

- $L_e = \varnothing$ and $L_n = \{L_{n-in}, L_{n-ex}\}$. $L_{n-in} = \varnothing$. $L_{n-ex} = \{type, counter\}$. **counter** is between 0 and the number of neighbours of each node. **type** = {N, NE, E}. **N** indicates that the sensor is not yet classified a leader or not a leader. **NE** indicates that the sensor is not a leader. **E** indicates that the sensor is a leader.
- $R_i = \varnothing$. $R_e = \{R1, R2\}$. These two rules are presented in Fig. 6.
- $I = \{N, d\}$. Because initially, type = {N} and counter = d with d is the degree of a node. The node degree is the number of tree edges connected to this node.

Every node of the network has a label **type** initialised to N and, after the election, exactly one node called the leader, should change this value to E. All other nodes should have the value NE.

The first rule in Fig. 6 indicates that when two sensors communicate, one having the label **counter** equals to one and the other his label **counter** is greater than one, then both of these sensors must decrease their label **counter**. When the **counter** of one of them reaches zero, then this sensor changes its label **type** to **NB** indicating that this sensor is not a leader. The second rule indicates that the last communicating pair of sensors (when the label **counter** equals to one, it indicates that it is the last neighbour to communicate with), one of them will be a leader i.e. changes its label **type** to **E** and the other sensor not a leader i.e. changes its label **type** to **NE**. An execution of the algorithm consists in applying the two relabelling rules until no rule is applicable.

5.2   Dead Animals Detection Algorithm

As a second example of a WSN distributed algorithm, we have the algorithm called dead animals detection Algorithm. Thus, we have sensors placed on animals. Each sensor allows measuring the temperature value of its attached animal.

Consequently, these sensors allow to detect if the animal is alive or dead. We suppose that the animals are always in the same place. The different sensors communicate together to exchange the collected information. When executing this algorithm the alert state is marked on all sensors if the number of dead animals reaches a threshold called **n**, **n** should be less than or equal to the number of sensors.

The set of animals forms a static and complete graph (G). In this graph, the sensors are represented by nodes (V). These nodes are connected through communication links represented by edges (E) in this graph.

The algorithm is coded with the following relabelling system according to the model presented in [15]: $\mathbf{S} = \{L_n, L_e, R_e, R_i, I\}$

- $L_n = \{L_{n-in}, L_{n-ex}\}$ and $L_e = \varnothing$. $L_{n-in} = \{\text{Animal\_State}\}$. We have, **Animal_State** $= \{\text{alive, dead}\}$. $L_{n-ex} = \{\text{counter, system\_state}\}$. **counter** is between 0 and animals_number, it is used for counting the number of dead animals. **system_state** $= \{\text{normal, alert}\}$. **system_state** becomes alert if the number of dead animals reaches the threshold n.
- $R_i = \{R1, R2\}$. $R_e = \{R3, R4, R5\}$. These rules are presented in Fig. 7. To simplify the figure, nodes with label system_state = alert are presented with empty (non coloured) nodes. Also, nodes with the label system_state = normal are presented with full (coloured) nodes.
- $I = \{\text{alive, 0, normal}\}$. Because initially, Animal_State $= \{\text{alive}\}$, counter $= 0$ and system_state $= \{\text{normal}\}$.

Thus, this algorithm operates as follows: if a sensor detects an elevation of its captured temperature value, then it changes its label from alive to dead by executing R1. R1 allows to change the label **Animal_State** from alive to dead and to add the node to the counter that contains the number of dead animals (**C**). R2 does the same as R1. However, it expresses the exception of R1: when the counter will reach n, the node will be in an alert state. When two sensors communicate together one of them will have the sum of counters (the number of dead animals in the graph), this is realised using R3. R4 does the same as R3. However, it expresses the exception of R3: when the sum of the two counters will reach n, the two nodes become on alert state. R5 expresses the spread of the alert state: when a node on alert state communicates with another node not informed by the alert state, the second will be marked also by the alert state. So, the algorithm works on collecting the number of dead animals by one node!; When this node detects that the number of dead animals in the network reaches the defined threshold, it will announce the alert state in the network. In this case, the execution of the algorithm will work on propagating the alert to all the nodes until all the nodes are informed (no rule is applied).

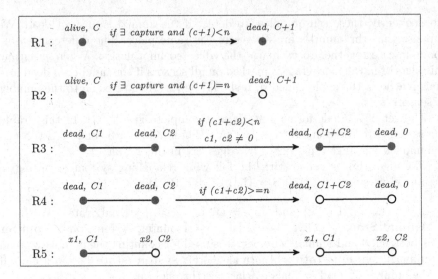

Fig. 7. Rules of dead animals algorithm

6 Simulation Results

In order to evaluate our WSN-HS algorithm presented as Algorithm 3, we compare it to the ATH algorithm in [9] presented as Algorithm 2. On one hand, we simulate the ATH algorithm with the leader election in a tree algorithm and with the dead animals detection algorithm. On the other hand, we simulate our WSN-HS algorithm with the leader election in a tree algorithm and with the dead animals algorithm and we compare the gathered results. In fact, in the dead animals algorithm, we explicitly consider a complete graph in order to compare the performance of our algorithm with a complete and a non-complete graph. The simulation of the handshake algorithms was realised using the CupCarbon simulator. The CupCarbon[1] is a smart city and Internet Of Things WSN Simulator. In fact, with CupCarbon [5], networks can be designed and prototyped by an ergonomic and easy interface using the OpenStreetMap (OSM) framework to deploy sensors directly on the map. CupCarbon includes a script called SenScript, which allows to program and to configure each sensor node individually. From this script, it is also possible to generate codes for hardware platforms such as Arduino/XBee.

Unlike most of the existing simulators, CupCarbon does not require an important previous knowledge in WSNs to understand their operation as mentioned in [11].

---

[1] http://www.cupcarbon.com/.

6.1 The Leader Election in a Tree Algorithm: With ATH Algorithm vs with WSN-HS Algorithm

In order to simulate the leader election in a tree algorithm with both handshake algorithms, we use the simulation parameters in CupCarbon presented in Table 1. We used 100 sensors with 20 sensors having a low energy level. A low energy level is lower than the defined threshold i.e., lower than 30% of the total energy level of a sensor. In this simulation, sensors consume energy only for communications and calculations and they do not capture environmental values. The radio module is based on Zigbee. In this simulation, the network has a tree topology. We executed this leader election algorithm 10 times with the ATH algorithm. Also, we realised 10 execution iterations of the leader election algorithm with our WSN-HS algorithm.

Table 1. Simulation parameters of Leader election in tree algorithm

Parameters	Simulation parameters value
Number of sensors	100
Number of sensors with residual energy < threshold	20
Energy threshold	30% of the total energy of a sensor

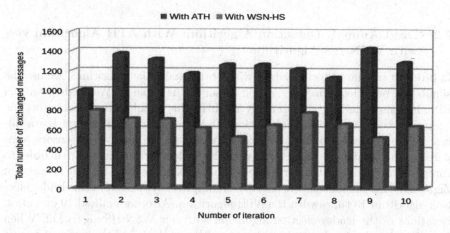

Fig. 8. Number of exchanged messages by the 20 sensors with low energy with ATH algorithm vs with WSN-HS algorithm (leader election algorithm)

When executing the leader election algorithm with the ATH algorithm on one side and with our WSN-HS algorithm on the other side, we collect the results shown in Fig. 8. This figure shows that when using our WSN-HS algorithm, the number of exchanged messages by the sensors having low energy is reduced.

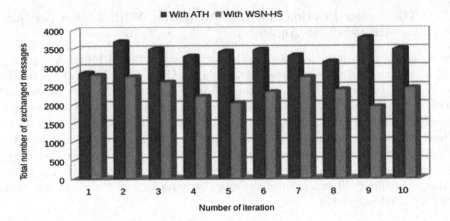

Fig. 9. Number of exchanged messages in the WSN with ATH algorithm vs with WSN-HS algorithm (leader election algorithm)

Precisely, when using our WSN-HS with the algorithm of leader election, we reduce the number of exchanged messages by the sensors having a low energy level by 47.1% comparing to the ATH algorithm. Moreover, the total number of exchanged messages is reduced for all the sensors in the network compared to the ATH algorithm by 28.7% as evinced by Fig. 9. As a consequence, the execution time is decreased by 20.6%.

6.2 Dead Animals Detection Algorithm: With ATH Algorithm vs with WSN-HS Algorithm

In order to simulate this algorithm with both handshake algorithms, we use the simulation parameters in CupCarbon presented in Table 2. We used 50 sensors with 10 sensors having a low energy level. In this simulation, sensors consume energy for communications, calculations and for capturing the temperature values of the attached animals. We explicitly change the number of sensors compared to the number of sensors used with the leader election algorithm in order to compare the results with different sizes of networks. The radio module is based on Zigbee. In this simulation, the network is complete. We executed this leader election algorithm 10 times with the ATH algorithm. Also, we realised 10 execution iterations of the leader election algorithm with our WSN-HS algorithm. When executing the dead animals detection algorithm with the ATH algorithm on one side and with our WSN-HS algorithm on the other side, we collect the results presented in Fig. 10. This figure shows that when using our WSN-HS algorithm, the number of exchanged messages by the sensors having low energy is significantly reduced. Precisely, when using WSN-HS algorithm with the algorithm of dead animals detection, we reduce the number of exchanged messages by the sensors having low energy by 94% compared to ATH algorithm. Moreover, the total number of exchanged messages is reduced for all the sensors in the network

Table 2. Simulation parameters of dead animals algorithm

Parameters	Simulation parameters value
Number of sensors	50
Number of sensors with residual energy < threshold	10
Energy threshold	30% of the total energy of a sensor

by 75% comparing to ATH algorithm as highlighted in Fig. 11. This improvement is realised due to the nature of the considered network. As expressed in the previous Section, we consider that the network is modelled as a complete graph. Ergo, there is a huge number of messages to exchange by the handshake algorithm because each sensor has 49 neighbours. With the ATH algorithm, in order to make two sensors communicate, each of them must choose the other from 49 neighbours. This procedure consumes a lot of energy and messages until they will choose each other. In fact, this is by dint of the low probability for them to choose each other from 49 neighbours. With our WSN-HS algorithm, we make this procedure much easier especially for sensors with low energy. In WSN-HS algorithm, sensors with low energy accept automatically the synchronisation of the sensor that sends a demand if they have enough energy to communicate with this latter. Furthermore, when any sensor accepts the synchronisation with a sensor directly from the waiting list, both of them avoid the problem of sending a huge number of messages to do a handshake. For this reason, in Fig. 12, we notice that the energy level decreased rapidly when using ATH algorithm in contrast to our WSN-HS algorithm.

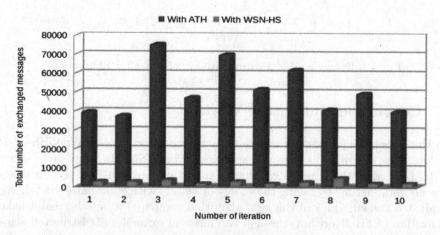

Fig. 10. Number of exchanged messages by 10 sensors with low energy with ATH algorithm vs with WSN-HS algorithm (dead animals detection algorithm)

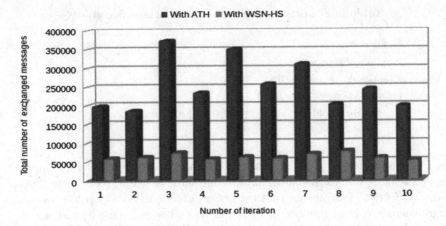

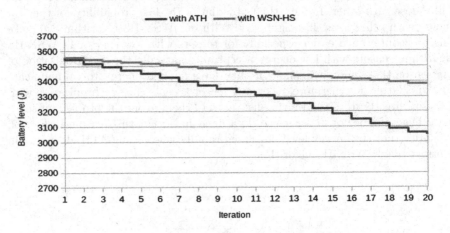

Fig. 11. Number of exchanged messages in the WSN with ATH algorithm vs with WSN-HS algorithm (dead animals detection algorithm)

Fig. 12. Energy level of a sensor with low energy after 10 iterations

7 Conclusion and Future Work

In this paper, we proposed a new handshake algorithm dubbed WSN-HS algorithm. This algorithm is designed specifically for WSNs. In contrast to other handshake algorithms, our algorithm is energy-efficient. In fact, it maximises the network lifetime by saving the energy of sensors with a low battery level. We evaluated the efficiency of this new algorithm compared to another handshake algorithm (ATH algorithm) through two different examples of distributed algorithms. The first algorithm is the leader election in a tree topology. In fact, the election algorithms are widely used for WSNs. The second algorithm is more specific for WSNs, it allows to spread the alert state on all sensors when the number of dead animals reaches a defined threshold. When testing these two algorithms with both our new and the existing handshake algorithm, we reach promising results. The simulation made by the CupCarbon simulator shows that our WSN-HS algorithm minimises the number of exchanged messages in the WSN for both distributed algorithms. Consequently, the energy consumption is minimised by our WSN-HS algorithm compared to the ATH algorithm. In addition to energy efficiency, the fault tolerance issue has immense practical importance in real sensor networks. This fact spurred us to make our algorithm not only energy-efficient but also fault-tolerant to sensors disappearance.

As future work, we aim at broadening the types of WSN on which our algorithm can be applied. For example, we can consider heterogeneous WSNs, dynamic WSNs and WSNs where sensors use renewable energies to recharge their batteries.

References

1. Abdallah, N.O., Kacem, H.H., Mosbah, M., Zemmari, A.: Broadcast in wireless mobile sensor networks with population protocols and extension with the rendezvous model. In: NOTERE, pp. 219–226. IEEE (2010)
2. Amiri, E., Keshavarz, H., Fahleyani, A.S., Moradzadeh, H., Komaki, S.: New algorithm for leader election in distributed WSN with software agents. In: 2013 IEEE International Conference on Space Science and Communication (IconSpace), pp. 290–295, July 2013. https://doi.org/10.1109/IconSpace2013.6599483
3. Angluin, D., Aspnes, J., Diamadi, Z., Fischer, M.J., Peralta, R.: Computation in networks of passively mobile finite-state sensors. Distrib. Comput. **18**(4), 235–253 (2006). https://doi.org/10.1007/s00446-005-0138-3
4. Aspnes, J., Ruppert, E.: An Introduction to Population Protocols, pp. 97–120. Springer, Berlin (2009). https://doi.org/10.1007/978-3-540-89707-1_5
5. Bounceur, A., et al.: CupCarbon: a new platform for the design, simulation and 2D/3D visualization of radio propagation and interferences in IoT networks. In: 2018 15th IEEE Annual Consumer Communications Networking Conference (CCNC), pp. 1–4, January 2018. https://doi.org/10.1109/CCNC.2018.8319179
6. Casteigts, A., Métivier, Y., Robson, J.M., Zemmari, A.: Design patterns in beeping algorithms: examples, emulation, and analysis. Inf. Comput. **264**, 32–51 (2019). https://doi.org/10.1016/j.ic.2018.10.001
7. Delporte-Gallet, C., Fauconnier, H., Guerraoui, R., Ruppert, E.: When birds die: making population protocols fault-tolerant. In: Gibbons, P.B., Abdelzaher, T., Aspnes, J., Rao, R. (eds.) DCOSS 2006. LNCS, vol. 4026, pp. 51–66. Springer, Heidelberg (2006). https://doi.org/10.1007/11776178_4
8. El Hibaoui, A., Métivier, Y., Robson, J.M., Saheb-Djahromi, N., Zemmari, A.: Analysis of a randomized dynamic timetable handshake algorithm. Pure Math. Appl. (Algebra Theor. Comput. Sci.) **18**(2), (2009). https://hal.archives-ouvertes.fr/hal-00376108
9. Fontaine, A., Mosbah, M., Tounsi, M., Zemmari, A.: A fault-tolerant handshake algorithm for local computations. In: AINA Workshops, pp. 475–480. IEEE Computer Society (2016)
10. Litovsky, I., Sopena, E.: Graph relabelling systems and distributed algorithms. In: Handbook of Graph Grammars and Computing by Graph Transformation, pp. 1–56. World Scientific (2001)

11. Lopez-Pavon, C., Sendra, S., Valenzuela-Valdés, J.F.: Evaluation of cupcarbon network simulator for wireless sensor networks. Netw. Protoc. Algorithms **10**(2), 1–27 (2018)
12. Métivier, Y., Saheb, N., Zemmari, A.: Analysis of a randomized rendezvous algorithm. Inf. Comput. **184**(1), 109–128 (2003). https://doi.org/10.1016/S0890-5401(03)00054-3
13. Métivier, Y., Sopena, E.: Graph relabelling systems: a general overview. Comput. Artif. Intell. **16**(2), 167–185 (1997)
14. Neamatollahi, P., Naghibzadeh, M., Abrishami, S., Yaghmaee, M.: Distributed clustering-task scheduling for wireless sensor networks using dynamic hyper round policy. IEEE Trans. Mob. Comput. **17**(2), 334–347 (2018). https://doi.org/10.1109/TMC.2017.2710050
15. Taktak, E., Tounsi, M., Mosbah, M., Kacem, A.H.: Distributed computations in wireless sensor networks by local interactions. In: Montavont, N., Papadopoulos, G.Z. (eds.) ADHOC-NOW 2018. LNCS, vol. 11104, pp. 293–304. Springer, Cham (2018). https://doi.org/10.1007/978-3-030-00247-3_26
16. Taktak, E., Tounsi, M., Mosbah, M., Kacem, A.H.: Proving distributed algorithms for wireless sensor networks by combining refinement and local computations. In: WETICE, pp. 217–222. IEEE Computer Society (2018)

Inter-slice Mobility Management in the Context of SDN/NFV Networks

Amal Kammoun[1,2(✉)], Nabil Tabbane[1], Gladys Diaz[2], Nadjib Achir[2],
and Abdulhalim Dandoush[3]

[1] MEDIATRON Laboratory, University of Carthage, Sup'Com, Aryanah, Tunisia
{amal.kammoun,nabil.tabbane}@supcom.tn
[2] L2TI Laboratory, University of Paris 13, Paris, France
{gladys.diaz,nadjib.achir}@univ-paris13.fr
[3] ESME, Paris, France
dandoush@esme.fr

Abstract. *Software Defined Networking (SDN)*, *Network Function Virtualization (NFV)* and *Network Slicing* technologies present promising solutions to enhance vehicular networks. Using these technologies, a dedicated slice will be deployed whenever a new service is requested. However, in this context, mobility management should be considered in order to support seamless roaming among different network slices. The roaming of users requires inter-slices interactions. In this paper, we propose a network slicing architecture for vehicular network application. We are interested especially in the management process. The challenge is to respect the required *Quality of Service (QoS)* for users during their movement from one slice to another. For this purpose, we propose an algorithm for the control of users' mobility between different network slices. *Mininet* emulator and *Ryu* controller were considered to validate our proposed algorithm.

Keywords: Handover · Network slicing · NFV · SDN · V2I · Mininet

1 Introduction

Fifth Generation Mobile Network (5G) aims to accommodate and respond to the stringent requirements of emergent use cases such as e-health and autonomous vehicles. The major problem of the traditional networks is the use of the *"one size fits all"* approach. This approach handles all types of services and users requirements over a single architecture, which causes a lack of flexibility and scalability. Thus, the vision of the 5G system is to migrate towards a horizontal approach. It aims to enhance the flexibility and agility of the network via the softwarization and the virtualization.

The softwarization and virtualization of networks are enabled through the *Software Defined Networking (SDN)* [1] and *Network Function Virtualization (NFV)* [2]. These technologies are complementary and ensure together high flexibility and programming for networks. In fact, the *SDN* separates the control

I. Jemili and M. Mosbah (Eds.): DiCES-N 2019, CCIS 1130, pp. 77–90, 2020.
https://doi.org/10.1007/978-3-030-40131-3_5

plane from the underlying infrastructure and moves the control logic to a centralized controller. Regarding *NFV*, it decouples *Network Functions (NFs)* from hardware resources to be implemented on virtual resources.

Enabled by *NFV* and *SDN*, *network slicing* is one of the most important features of 5G. This technology allows the provision of a dedicated network slice for each type of service. The *Network Slice* is defined as the composition of several chained *Virtual Network Functions (VNFs)* running on top of virtual machines and containers. *Network Slices* are created on users' demand and each slice is composed of *VNFs* that are required by the service.

In this paper, we are interested in the use case of vehicular network slices. Actually, thanks to *Global Positioning System (GPS)* and *Radio Detection and Ranging (RADAR)* the cooperative driving and the management of connected vehicles become more feasible. Moreover, connected cameras of vehicles enhance vehicles safety by providing information about road obstacles, conditions, and future moves.

Vehicular Ad-hoc Networks (VANETs) are considered as a promising network design for intelligent transportation systems [3]. They enable a class of applications that requires time-critical responses, very high data rates and a consideration of the very high mobility of vehicles. For instance, the Vehicle-to-Vehicle (V2V) and the Vehicle-to-Infrastructure (V2I) use cases require less than 10 ms latency. The architecture of VANETs, as shown in Fig. 1, is complex, inflexible and characterized by an absence of a centralized control which give rise to challenges in resource management, data scheduling and mobility management.

Therefore, a new network architecture models are required in order to manage the vehicles mobility and to respond to *VANET* service requirements especially in terms of reliability, availability and latency. In this context, the *SDN/NFV* paradigm presents an opportunity for a more flexible and programmable network [4].

In such a challenging context, we present in this paper our considered architecture to support vehicular network slices. The key idea of this architecture is the multi-level delegation for slice creation and management. It is a layered architecture that provides a control system and a network store for the management and provision of network services. The control system handles all the user requests, optimizes the system performances and programs the underlying virtual infrastructure with network functions and services. The network functions and services are stored in the network store layer and they are enclosed by *Over-The-Top third* parties and network operators.

We are interested also in the mobility management of vehicles between different slices. In fact, vehicles will be on a continuous moving from different zones. The considered architecture has to react to this mobility and ensure a seamless moving. Therefore, we propose an algorithm to handle the handover of vehicles from one slice to another based on the *Received Signal Strength (RSS)* and load situation of available slices.

The remainder of this paper is organized as follows: in the second section we present our related works. The third section presents our considered architecture and introduces our proposed algorithm for the mobility management. In section four, we present simulations and performances evaluation of the handover process. The last section concludes the paper and gives some perspectives.

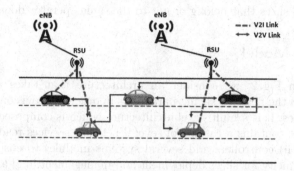

Fig. 1. VANET architecture

2   Related Works

The application of *SDN* in vehicular networks has recently been the focus of several researches. In [5], evaluation results demonstrate the benefits of SDN in managing a video streaming application over several wireless interfaces relying on V2V and V2I communications. In [6], authors propose a network architecture that enables the slicing function for vehicle network service and improves the bandwidth utilization. In [7], authors study the case of cooperative driving among autonomous vehicles. They propose a centralized resource management framework for the computing and storage resources on cloud-computing based on SDN and NFV control modules. In the literature, some works focused on the mobility management on the context of SDN networks. In [12], authors presents a survey on the management of the handover in the context of VANETs and 5G mobile networks. They highlight the limitations of existing handover solutions and how 5G solutions can handle them.

In [8] authors were interested in the application of SDN to aeronautical communications for traffic management purposes. In this context, they study the handover mechanism for video streaming application. In [9], authors propose a vertical handover decision algorithm in SDN context based on *Received Signal Strength (RSS)*, *bandwidth* and *delay*. Their aim is to enhance the delivered *QoS* to network users. In [11], authors propose a mobility management protocol for fast handover action using discrete-time Markov models. In [10], authors propose an architecture to support Vehicle-to-Everything (V2X) network slices. They study the handover decision with and without slice federation while considering the load state of target slices.

In our work, we propose a network architecture for the management of users' mobility. This architecture considers a multi-level control and orchestration to the provided services and network resources. In fact, a centralized SDN Controller for all the deployed slices increases the overhead messages in order to update the vehicle location. Thus, we consider a dedicated orchestrator for each deployed slice. Moreover, we study the perceived QoS at the user level when he moves between slices that belong or not to the same operator domain.

3   System Model

As depicted in Fig. 2, we consider an architecture that takes advantage of SDN/NFV and the network slicing paradigms in order to provision and manage end-to-end slices. It is a multi-level architecture which is composed of (i) a network store that contains a catalog of several network services ready to be used by the users, (ii) controllers and several systems modules to ensure optimization and dynamicity for slices deployment and management, and also to update needed information (resources and functions states), (iii) a set of slices that forward users' flows and (iv) servers and forwarding elements that constitute the virtual infrastructure.

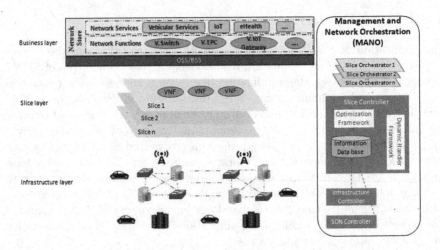

Fig. 2. Network slicing and management architecture

3.1   Business Layer

This layer encompasses the *Network Store* and the *Operations Support System/Business Support System (OSS/BSS)*.

The *OSS* and *BSS* ensure both the management and the orchestration of legacy network systems. They have a visibility of the provided services in the operator network domain.

The *Network Store* provides a catalog of use cases exposed to end users. It has the same utility as the application store for the software platform (e.g. App Store, Play Store, etc.). In fact, it provides a marketplace of *Network Functions (NF)*. Thanks to this marketplace, use cases will be supplied. Thus, following a user's request, appropriated *Virtual Network Functions (VNFs)* are chosen of this catalog to build the service chain. As an example of *Network Store*, we mention the project T-NOVA [13], which provides a marketplace for (VNFs).

As example of services we cite:

– The smart parking use case: it is one of the most popular *V2I* applications. Vehicles will retrieve data through sensors placed on the ground in order to find a vacant parking space. Controllers have a global view of all vehicles path and sensors location. Thus, the monitoring of road conditions in congestion and emergencies cases is more flexible and scalable.
– The video streaming sharing between vehicles: vehicles can share videos about the road to better understand their environment and anticipate the risk of collision. For this service, the *Infrastructure Controller* discovers, identifies and selects the nodes of the virtual network for the establishment of the service. It has to identify the nodes capable of transmitting the information (existence of an on-board video camera in the vehicle) and/or nodes capable of transferring the video.

3.2   Management and Network Orchestration

This layer controls and orchestrates the network resources, VNFs, and users' requests. It is composed of several blocks which are presented in the following parts.

1. The *Slice Orchestrator*: for each slice, a *Slice Orchestrator* is in charge of its end-to-end life-cycle and management. Basically, it communicates its slice information and its requests to the *Slice Controller*. It also implements controller commands and decisions (e.g. packet forwarding rules) into slices forwarding devices.
2. The *Slice Controller*: it is composed of fundamental modules that support the optimization of slices deployment and the management of events introducing changes in the behavior of deployed slices. In the following we define these modules.
   – *Optimization Framework*: it takes into consideration users requirements as well as the network system state in order to optimize the service chain creation, the VM allocation and the deployment of the slices over the network infrastructure. Also, this component determines whether the current slice is able to execute an additional request or not.

- *Dynamic Handler Framework (DHF)*: in order to deal with events that occur in the system such as the congestion of a slice, the failure of a VM implementation, the user mobility, etc., we need to monitor in real time the deployed slices. The *DHF* analyses periodically the information database and detects the trigger events for the addition, deletion and modification of slice resources.
- *Information Database*: this database gathers the information collected by the controllers. This information relates to several network aspects such as the current processing capacity of the servers, the available link bandwidths, the number of VMs per server and also the utilization rate of each slice. Controllers update this database periodically with new measurement.
- Slice Controller: it is responsible to execute several tasks such as the mapping of a new slice request to an already created slice, the assignment of a dedicated *Slice Orchestrator* for each created slice and the request of the creation of a new slice.

3. The *Infrastructure Controller* and *SDN Controller* are responsible for the control and the supervision of the entire underlying infrastructure (concerning compute and network resources). the *Infrastructure Controller* determines the resources that will be allocated for a slice while considering the state of the virtual infrastructure. It is also responsible for the programming of virtual machines with different network functions and services.

3.3   Slice Layer

The *Slice Layer* contains the set of the deployed slices over the underlying infrastructure. Each network slice is dedicated for a specific type of service. In this paper, we define a network slice as a customized virtual network running on top of a shared physical infrastructure that may cross several domains. It is composed of a set of connectivity (links), storage, and computing resources dedicated for one application to meet specific needs.

3.4   Virtual Infrastructure Layer

The *Virtual Infrastructure Layer* encompasses all software and hardware resources that form the virtual environment. It includes the connectivity between data centers and clouds systems as well as the computing, storage and network capabilities.

3.5   Slices Deployment Process

The slice deployment process consists on the implementation of VNFs on the corresponding virtual network resources as shown in Fig. 3. To set up this process, the *Service Provider* receives users' demands and according to their requirements it deploys a network slice that responds to their requests. The deployment of network slices is accompanied with a complete control and orchestration of the system operation and an optimization sub-system that aims to maximize the system performance and to optimize resource utilization.

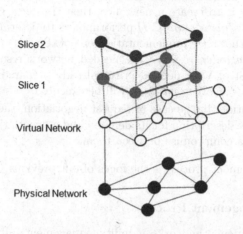

Fig. 3. Network slicing concept

According to our architecture presented in Fig. 2, we consider cars as the nodes of the virtual infrastructure. Network services are exposed to the drivers on a catalogue provided by the *Service Provider*.

Several steps are required for the slice deployment. Those steps start by the analysis of the user's request, then the creation of the slice description according to the user's requirements and finally the slice implementation. In the following we detail each of these steps.

1. Request analysis: when the user's demand is received, the system starts by defining the set of its requirements and also the information about the user profile in order to have a complete description of the user's request.
2. Slice description: after analyzing the request, the *Slice Controller* searches for an existing deployed slice that responds to this demand. Two cases can be considered:
   (a) first, the *Slice Controller* may find some deployed *VNFs* that can be reused for the user's request. In this case, the *Slice Controller* will study the performances of the *VNF* which will be reused. In [14], we have proposed an algorithm for the performance evaluation in terms of reliability, availability and latency. Therefore, if the performances of the founded *VNFs* are less than a fixed threshold then an additional demand may be served by those *VNFs*.
   (b) Second, the *Slice Controller* will create a new slice description while specifying the needed information for its implementation.
3. Slice Implementation: after defining the required operation for the user's request, two actions are possible.

(a) If the defined action is the reuse of some already implemented VNFs, then the *Slice Controller* will create a slice which is composed of the reused VNFs and the new created ones. After that, it will inform the *Slice Orchestrator* and the *Slice Service Orchestrator* about this new operation.

(b) If the action is to create a new slice, then the *Slice Controller* studies the *Virtual Infrastructure (VI)* performances to determine if it is able to support another slice implementation or not. So, the *Infrastructure and Network Controller* reserves the needed network resources and implements the list of VNF defined in the already prepared slice description. Otherwise, a *request negotiation* will be executed.

4. Request Negotiation: in the case of request negotiation, the system proposes to the user a new description for its demand and a negotiation will take place in order to find a compromise between them.

The slice deployment process is the focus of our previous works in [14, 15].

3.6 Slices Management Process

In the context of vehicular networks, mobility management and users roaming are complicated issues that require inter-slices interactions. The goal is to maintain the required QoS for the user when he moves from its home slice to the visited slice.

To perform the handover three phases are required as shown in Fig. 4. The first phase is the *Slice and Resources Information Gathering*. In this phase, the controllers collect the contextual information about all the available slices, determine the planned trajectory and actual position of vehicles and examine the users' requirements. The second phase is the handover decision. This phase determines the best moment to trigger the handover and chooses the most suitable target slice. The last phase is the handover execution. It consists on transferring the current session to the selected slice.

In order to determine the target slice and the accurate moment to perform the handover we propose a mobility management algorithm presented in Algorithm 1 . Our proposed algorithm will decide the need to perform the handover and when it should be initiated whereas vehicles are moving between network slices. The main interactions during handover action are presented in Fig. 5.

The *Dynamic Handler Framework* continuously monitors the *information data base*. It examines the status of the users' home slice, the planned trajectory and the actual position of the vehicles. This information will be used to determine if a vehicle needs a handover action or not and to which slice the handover will be performed. The *information data base* is updated by the *Infrastructure Controller*, *Slice Controller* and *SDN controller*. In our algorithm we consider the RSS value and load state of the network slices as well as the delivered QoS to the users in order to decide about the initiation of the handover as shown in Algorithm 1.

Whenever the *Dynamic Handler Framework* detects that a handover action should be performed, it notifies the *Slice Controller* which in its turn interacts with the corresponding *Slice Orchestrator*. The *Slice Orchestrator* of the home

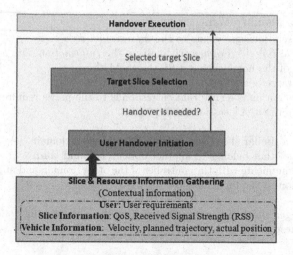

Fig. 4. Dynamic handler framework

slice communicates with the *Slice Orchestrator* of the target slice via their slice controllers to exchange the information about the service requirements of the vehicle.

The *Slice Controller* of the target slice will select a slice that corresponds to the user's requirements. If there is a slice that fits the user requirements, the user will be mapped to this slice. Otherwise, the slice that better suits the request is selected to host the user. Finally, the Slice Controller ensures the migration of the user's flows and updates the data base.

4   Simulations and Results

For our simulations, we use the Mininet-WiFi network emulator [16]. Mininet-WiFi is a fork of Mininet emulator with WiFi features. It allows the evaluation of wireless networks with OpenFlow switches and wireless access points. In our simulation, WiFi slices are considered. Emulated vehicles are multi-interfaces hosts that connect to both radio networks and access points. Ryu Controller was implemented in the system. It is a Python controller that supports OpenFlow 1.3.

As shown in Fig. 6, we consider in our simulation three overlapped slices. Slice 1 and slice 2 belong to the same slice provider. They are controlled by the same *Slice Controller*. However, the slice 3 belongs to another domain and it is controlled by another *Slice Controller*. At the beginning, the target vehicle is served by the slice 1. When it moves from the zone served by the first slice towards the zone served by the second slice, a handover to slice 2 should be performed. When the user will be served by the second slice, a migration of the routing information should be done by the slice controller [17]. Vehicles are running video streaming application during their mobility between slices. The video streaming traffic was simulated using the Iperf traffic generator. Parameters of our simulation are summarized in Table 1.

Algorithm 1. Mobility Management Process

1: Controllers send measurements to the *information data base*
2: The *Dynamic Handler Framework* analyzes the *Information data base*
3: **if** The RSS of the home slice < RSS threshold **then**
4:    Search a target slice
5:    **if** The system finds a slice that corresponds to the user's requirements **then**
6:       Migrate the user's session to this slice
7:    **else**
8:       Search a similar slice from another slice provider domain
9:       **if** A slice that belongs to another domain is found **then**
10:         Communicate with the controller of the other domain and migrate the user's session to the founded slice
11:      **else**
12:         Trigger the handover to the slice or the network that offers the closest requestet QoS
13:      **end if**
14:   **end if**
15:   **if** Load of the home slice > 80% **and** QoS delivered to the user decreases **then**
16:      **if** RSS target slice > RSS home slice **then**
17:         Trigger Handover
18:      **else**
19:         No handover
20:      **end if**
21:   **end if**
22: **end if**

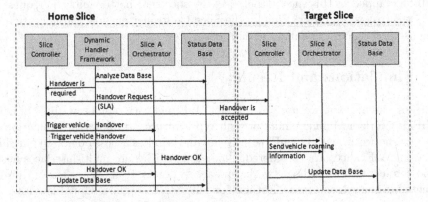

Fig. 5. Main interactions of the handover process

For our simulations, we evaluate the offered QoS to vehicles in terms of the throughput and end-to-end delay. The throughput is the rate at which packets are successfully received per unit of time. In the presented results, the throughput is measured in Mbit per second (Mbit/s). The end-to-end delay refers to the duration between the moment of the packet transmission and the moment of packet reception.

Table 1. Simulation parameters

Simulator	Mininet-WiFi
Controller	Ryu (OpenFlow 1.3)
Simulation duration	200 s
Number of vehicles at handover time	1, 5, 10
Vehicle velocity	10 m/s
Node starts moving at	0 s
Traffic starts at	1 s
Traffic type	Video streaming
Number of slices	3

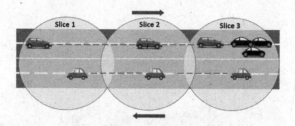

Fig. 6. Users mobility from one Slice to another

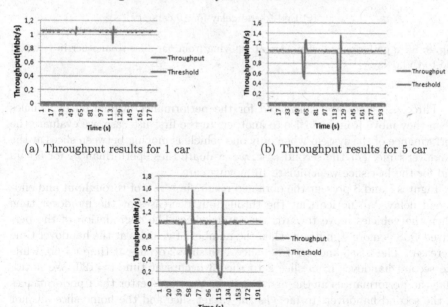

(a) Throughput results for 1 car

(b) Throughput results for 5 car

(c) Throughput results for 10 cars

Fig. 7. Slice performance when cars are moving from one slice to another in terms of throughput

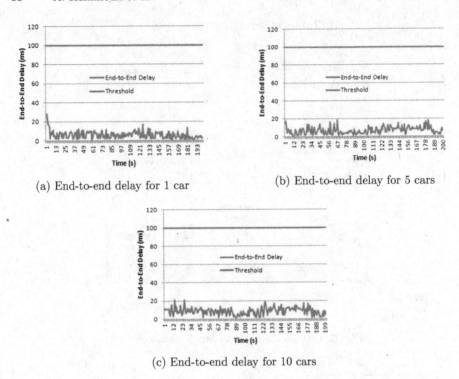

(a) End-to-end delay for 1 car

(b) End-to-end delay for 5 cars

(c) End-to-end delay for 10 cars

Fig. 8. Slice performance when cars are moving from one slice to another in terms of end-to-end delay

Three use cases are considered for the performance evaluation of vehicles when they move from one slice to another. In the first use case, we evaluate the performance of the system when only one vehicle is moving between slices at the handover time. For the second case, we evaluate these performances for 5 cars and for the last slice we simulate 10 moving cars.

Figures 7 and 8 present the obtained results in terms of throughput and end-to-end delay. We notice that the throughput decreases at the handover time when the vehicles move towards the target slice. The degradation of the perceived QoS is more significant when the number of vehicles at the handover time increases. The first handover from slice 1 to slice 2 occurs at time $t = 60$, while the second handover from slice 2 to slice 3 occurs at time $t = 120$. We notice that the performances at the first handover time are better than performances in the second handover. In fact, as the target slice and the home slice are not controlled by the same controller, an additional latency will occur in the system for the handover of vehicles. For both handover cases, throughput results are higher than the threshold defined for video streaming applications in [18]. For the end-to-end delay results, we notice that this value is not affected by the handover action for the two cases. This value is always lower than the threshold.

5   Conclusion

Mobility is a critical aspect in vehicular networks and it affects the Quality of Service delivered to the users. In this work, we are interested in the mobility management in the context of network slices. We propose a handover algorithm for the decision of the handover execution and the selection of the target slice. We study the performances of running services during the handover time when vehicles roam between slices under different load scenarios.

As future works, we plan to study the scalability issue and evaluate the handover performances with ONOS and OpenDayLight controllers. Furthermore, we aim to consider other handover criteria like the energetic cost and the vehicle velocity for a better handover decision. We manage also to include other divisional techniques like the fuzzy logic and reinforcement learning to better take the handover decision.

References

1. Kreutz, D., Ramos, F.M.V., Veríssimo, P.E., Rothenberg, C.E., Azodolmolky, S., Uhlig, S.: Software-defined networking: a comprehensive survey. In: Proceedings of the IEEE, vol. 103, pp. 14–76, January 2015
2. Mijumbi, R., Serrat, J., Gorricho, J.L., Bouten, N., Turck, F.D., Boutaba, R.: Network function virtualization: state-of-the-art and research challenges. IEEE Commun. Surv. Tutorials **18**, 236–262 (2016)
3. Cunha, F., et al.: Data communication in VANETS: protocols, applications and challenges. Ad Hoc Netw. **44**, 90–103 (2016)
4. Shah, S.A.A., Ahmed, E., Imran, M., Zeadally, S.: 5G for vehicular communications. IEEE Commun. Mag. **56**, 111–117 (2018)
5. Fontes, R.D.R., Campolo, C., Rothenberg, C.E., Molinaro, A.: From theory to experimental evaluation: resource management in software-defined vehicular networks. IEEE Access **5**, 3069–3076 (2017)
6. Gu, R., Zhang, S., Ji, Y., Yan, Z.: Network slicing and efficient onu migration for reliable communications in converged vehicular and fixed access network. Veh. Commun. **11**, 57–67 (2018)
7. Peng, H., Ye, Q., Shen, X.: SDN-based resource management for autonomous vehicular networks: a multi-access edge computing approach, CoRR, vol. abs/1809.08966 (2018)
8. Luong, D.K., Ali, M., Benamrane, F., Ammar, I., Hu, Y.-F.: Seamless handover for video streaming over an SDN-based aeronautical communications network. SIGMETRICS Perform. Eval. Rev. **46**, 98–99 (2019)
9. Rizkallah, J., Akkari, N.: SDN-based vertical handover decision scheme for 5G networks. In: 2018 IEEE Middle East and North Africa Communications Conference (MENACOMM), pp. 1–6, April 2018
10. Campolo, C., Fontes, R.D.R., Molinaro, A., Rothenberg, C.E., Iera, A.: Slicing on the road: enabling the automotive vertical through 5G network softwarization. Sensors **18**(12), 4435 (2018)
11. Fafolahan, E.M.O., Pierre, S.: A seamless mobility management protocol in 5G locator identificator split dense small cells. IEEE Trans. Mob. Comput. 1 (2019)

12. Ahmed, A.A., Alzahrani, A.A.: A comprehensive survey on handover management for vehicular ad hoc network based on 5G mobile networks technology. Trans. Emerg. Telecommun. Technol. **30**(3), e3546 (2019)

13. Xilouris, G., et al.: T-NOVA: a marketplace for virtualized network functions. In: 2014 European Conference on Networks and Communications (EuCNC), pp. 1–5, June 2014

14. Kammoun, A., Tabbane, N., Diaz, G., Dandoush, A., Achir, N.: End-to-end efficient heuristic algorithm for 5G network slicing. In: 2018 IEEE 32nd International Conference on Advanced Information Networking and Applications (AINA), pp. 386–392, May 2018

15. Kammoun, A., Tabbane, N., Diaz, G., Achir, N.: Admission control algorithm for network slicing management in SDN-NFV environment. In: 2018 6th International Conference on Multimedia Computing and Systems (ICMCS), pp. 1–6, May 2018

16. Mininet-wifi. https://github.com/intrig-unicamp/mininet-wifi. Accessed 25 Aug 2019

17. Zhao, Y., Lo, S., Zegura, E., Riga, N., Ammar, M.: Virtual Network Migration on the GENI Wide-Area SDN-Enabled Infrastructure, arXiv e-prints, arXiv:1701.01702, January 2017

18. ITU-T-Rec. G.1010: End-user Multimedia QoS Categories, Technical report, International Telecommunication Union (2001)

On a New Quantization Algorithm for Secondary User Scheduling in 5G Network

Ayman Massaoudi[1,2]([✉]) [iD], Noura Sellami[3] [iD], and Mohamed Siala[2] [iD]

[1] Department of Computer Science, Jouf University, Sakakah, Saudi Arabia
ahmassaaoudi@ju.edu.sa
[2] MEDIATRON Laboratory, Sup'Com, Carthage University, Ariana, Tunisia
{aymen.massaoudi,mohamed.siala}@supcom.tn
[3] LETI Laboratory, ENIS, Sfax University, Sfax, Tunisia
noura.sellami@enis.tn

Abstract. Opportunistic beamforming (OB) has been investigated in the 5th generation (5G) network to jointly maximize the sum rate of the secondary network and minimize the interference induced to the primary users. In this paper, we consider the cognitive radio context and we investigate the problem of SINR (signal to interference plus noise ratio) quantization in secondary network. Based on OB, we propose a suitable quantization scheme that minimizes the secondary system throughput loss due to the quantization. Via theoretical analysis and Matlab simulations, we demonstrate that our proposed algorithm attains maximum sum rate and outperforms others schemes proposed in the literature.

Keywords: 5th generation · Opportunistic beamforming · Cognitive radio · Users scheduling · Adaptive SINR quantization · Fairness

1 Introduction

In the 5th generation (5G) networks, cognitive radio (CR) is one of the promising techniques for efficient spectrum utilization in wireless systems. CR allows unlicensed users to share the radio frequency (RF) spectrum with the licensed (primary) users (see for example [1–7] and references therein). We study, in this work, an *underlay* cognitive radio (CR) system in secondary users co-exist with a licensed user (LU). Based on opportunistic beamforming (OB) [8], the multi-antennas secondary base station (SBS) uses a scheduling algorithm of the cognitive users (CUs) consisting of two steps. In the first phase, we choose the beams that mitigate the interference caused to the LU. In the second phase, the SINR (signal to interference plus noise ratio) is calculated by the CUs for each beam. Then, the maximum SINR (MSINR) for each CU and the corresponding beam identifier are sent back to the SBS. The latter chooses for transmission the CUs having the greatest MSINRs. Practically, for the sake of efficiently use

© Springer Nature Switzerland AG 2020
I. Jemili and M. Mosbah (Eds.): DiCES-N 2019, CCIS 1130, pp. 91–101, 2020.
https://doi.org/10.1007/978-3-030-40131-3_6

of the limited power and bandwidth, every CU sends back to the transmitter a quantized version of its maximum SINR.

In the literature, the SINR quantization for non-cognitive systems based on opportunistic beamforming (OB) has been investigated [9–13]. For instance, in [9] author proposed to use the pdf matched quantization in order to minimize the sum rate distortion, and analyzed the impact of the feed-back quantization on the system throughput. Authors in [12] studied the problem of limited feed-back for block diagonalization precoded MIMO (multiple input multiple output) broadcast channels. In order to obtain a multi-user diversity gain, Moon *et al.* proposed a quantization technique based on a derivation of the received SINR by calculating the average received SINR for every user. In [13], Panda *et al.* considered two approaches of using the threshold to determine the quantization levels. In the first approach a fixed threshold is considered for all set of users. In the second approach, Panda *et al.* proposed an adaptive threshold technique in which the threshold values are determined depending on the number of users.

Nevertheless, the context of this work is different since it deals with cognitive radio network. In [5], authors considered the cognitive context and proposed to quantize the SINR feed-back based on the Lloyd Max quantizer [14]. However, the Lloyd Max algorithm suffers from convergence to local minima and can not always find the optimal quantizer.

In this paper, we propose a new quantizer scheme suitable for the scheduling algorithm of [2] which reduces the secondary system throughput loss owing to the SINR quantization. We determine the set of quantization thresholds and we develop a statistical analysis for the impact of the proposed quantizer on the throughput of the cognitive system. We also address the fairness issue of our proposed scheduling scheme.

The rest of the paper is divided into following sections. In Sect. 2, we present the system model and the cognitive users scheduling scheme studied in this work. In Sect. 3, we explain our proposed quantization scheme , and we evaluate it in Sect. 4. In Sect. 5, we conclude the paper.

2   A Quantization-Based Cognitive Users Scheduling

In this section, we describe the cognitive system model. As shown in Fig. 1, a cognitive (unlicensed) network share the spectrum with a primary (licensed) network.

1. The secondary network composed of:
   - a SBS having M antennas, and
   - K cognitive users ($M \ll K$). Each secondary receiver has a single antenna.
2. The licensed network composed of:
   - one user, and
   - a licensed base station (LBS).

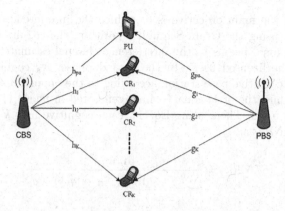

Fig. 1. Cognitive radio network model

We note here, that the PU and the PBS are equipped with a single antenna each. We are concerned with the downlink of the secondary system in which independent signals are transmitted by the SBS to N_s scheduled CUs, $1 \leq N_s \leq M - 1$. The received signal at the k-th ($1 \leq k \leq K$) unlicensed user can be derived as:

$$y_k = \sqrt{P_s} \mathbf{h}_k \sum_{i \in \mathbb{S}} \mathbf{w}_i x_i + \sqrt{P_{pu}} g_k x_{pu} + n_k, \tag{1}$$

where:

- $\mathbb{S}$ denotes the set of the N_s selected CUs,
- P_s (resp. P_{pu}) is the transmitted power for each selected CU (resp. for the LU). Notice that we adopt equal power allocation.
- $\mathbf{h}_k = [h_{k,1}, h_{k,2}, \cdots, h_{k,M}]$, for $1 \leq k \leq K$ and $1 \leq m \leq M$, where $h_{k,m}$ is the channel gain between the m-th transmit antenna of the secondary base station and the k-th CU.
- $\mathbf{g} = [g_1, g_2, \cdots, g_K]$, where g_k, is the channel tap gain between the primary base station and the k-th CU receive antenna. Notice that $\mathbf{g}$ and $\mathbf{h}_k$ are i.i.d.[1] complex Gaussian samples of a random variable with mean equal to 0 and variance equal to1.
- $\mathbf{w}_i$ is the beamforming weight vector (of size $M \times 1$) for the i-th selected cognitive user.
- x_i (resp. x_{pu}) denotes the data transmitted from the SBS to the i-th cognitive user (resp. from the primary base station to the licensed user),
- n_k represents the noise at the k-th CU. n_k is a Gaussian random variable with zero mean and variance σ_k^2.

In this work, we assume that the FDD[2] mode is used and we are concerned with the two-phases secondary users scheduling algorithm proposed in [2]. In

---

[1] independent and identically distributed.
[2] Frequency Division Duplex.

the first phase, the main objective is to reduce the interference caused to the PU. Indeed, by using the Gram Schmidt algorithm, the cognitive base station generates orthogonal beams to the interference channel estimate (link between the SBS and the licensed user). In the second phase, N_s cognitive users are selected by the cognitive base station according to the opportunistic beamforming (OB) [8]. Thus, the orthogonal beams (generated in phase 1.) are broadcast to all cognitive users. Then, using Eq. (1), each cognitive user k computes the following N_s SINRs as:

$$SINR_{k,j} = \frac{|\mathbf{h}_k \mathbf{w}_j|^2}{\sum_{i=1,\, i \neq j}^{N_s} |\mathbf{h}_k \mathbf{w}_i|^2 + \alpha\, |g_k|^2 + \rho_k}, \tag{2}$$

where:

- $\alpha = \frac{P_{pu}}{P_s}$,
- $\rho_k = \frac{P_s}{\sigma_k^2}$: the SNR (signal to noise ratio) of the kth cognitive user.

We suppose that, using training, each cognitive receiver k knows $\mathbf{h}_k \mathbf{w}_i$, for $1 \leq i \leq N_s$. Consequently, the k-th CU is able to accurately calculate the SINRs based on the above Eq. (2). According to conventional OB [8], each user sends back to the SBS the value of its maximum SINR (MSINR) together with the corresponding beam index. In our work, we take into account the practical case where every unlicensed user sends back its maximum SINR quantized to the SBS. Indeed, the cognitive base station divides the value range of MSINR into $Q = 2^b$ intervals. The boundaries values of these intervals are assumed to be known for each CU and given by: $b_0 < b_1 < \ldots < b_Q$. For a given unlicensed user k, we denote by $\gamma_k^{N_s} \leq \cdots \leq \gamma_k^u \leq \cdots \leq \gamma_k^1$ the ordered SINRs. Thus, for the k-th cognitive user, if its largest SINR value (γ_k^1) is in the q-th interval ($1 \leq q \leq Q$), i.e. $b_{q-1} < \gamma_k^1 \leq b_q$, it will feed back the indicator q of the interval with the indicator of its best beam. Then, the cognitive base station assigns the beams to elected cognitive users on the basis of the feed-back information.

More precisely, there are two possibilities for a given beam:

- the beam is chosen by at least one CU (**Hypothesis** $\mathcal{H}_1$),
- or no CU requests this beam (**Hypothesis** $\mathcal{H}_0$). In this case, it is assigned to a CU at random.

In this paper, we study the throughput loss due to the SINR quantization and we propose a new quantization scheme that minimizes this loss.

3   Proposed Quantization Scheme

Throughout this section, the proposed quantization scheme is described. Then, we compare our proposed quantizer to the one proposed in [9].

In this work, the proposed quantizer is designed in order to minimize the throughput loss R_{loss}, given by:

$$R_{loss} = R_A - R_Q$$

where R_A(resp. R_Q) represents the throughput of the cognitive system with analog feed-back (resp. throughput of the cognitive system with quantized feed-back).

Let the occurrence probabilities of hypotheses $\mathcal{H}_0$ and $\mathcal{H}_1$ be $P_{\mathcal{H}_0}$ and $P_{\mathcal{H}_1}$ respectively. Hence, R_A can be written as:

$$R_A \simeq N_s \left(P_{\mathcal{H}_1} \int_0^{+\infty} \log_2 (1 + \gamma)\, p_1(\gamma)\, d\gamma \right.$$

$$\left. + P_{\mathcal{H}_0} \int_0^{+\infty} \log_2 (1 + \gamma)\, p_0(\gamma)\, d\gamma \right), \tag{3}$$

where:

- $p_1(\gamma)$ denotes the probability density function (pdf) of the MSINR for a given transmitted beam. We express the pdf of the MSINR as [2]:

$$p_1(\gamma) = K f_s(\gamma)\, (F_s(\gamma))^{K-1}, \tag{4}$$

where

- $f_s(\gamma)$ represents the pdf of $SINR_{k,j}$ in Eq. (2), and can be written as:

$$f_s(\gamma) = \sum_{j=1}^{N_s-1} \frac{a_j \exp(-\gamma/\rho_k)}{(\gamma+1)^{j+1}} \left(\frac{\gamma+1}{\rho_k} + j \right) \tag{5}$$

$$+ \frac{a_{N_s} \exp(-\gamma/\rho_k)}{(\alpha\gamma+1)^2} \left(\frac{\alpha\gamma+1}{\rho_k} + \alpha \right),$$

- $F_s(\gamma)$ represents the cdf of $SINR_{k,j}$ in (2), and can be written as:

$$F_S(\gamma) = 1 - \left(\sum_{j=1}^{N_s-1} \frac{a_j \exp(-\gamma/\rho)}{(\gamma+1)^j} + \frac{a_{N_s} \exp(-\gamma/\rho)}{(\alpha\gamma+1)} \right), \tag{6}$$

where a_j, for $1 \le j \le N_s$, are constants.

- $p_0(\gamma)$ represents the pdf of the largest SINR per CU and can be written as [5]:

$$p_0(\gamma) = \frac{N_s}{\alpha(N_s-2)!} \sum_{i=0}^{N_s-1} \binom{N_s-1}{i} (-1)^i \sum_{j=0}^{N_s-2} \binom{N_s-2}{j}$$

$$\times \frac{(-i\gamma)^j}{(\gamma+\frac{1}{\alpha})^{j+1}} \exp\left(-\frac{\gamma}{\rho_k} \left(1 + \frac{i(\gamma+1)}{1-i\gamma} \right) \right) \sum_{d=0}^{N_s-2-j} \binom{N_s-2-j}{d}$$

$$\times (1-i\gamma)^d \left(-\frac{i\gamma}{\rho_k} \right)^{N_s-2-j-d} \left(\Sigma_{i,j,d}^1(\gamma) + \Sigma_{i,j,d}^2(\gamma) \right) U(1-i\gamma) \tag{7}$$

where:

- $\Sigma^1_{i,j,d}(\gamma) = \sum_{l=0}^{d}\left(\dfrac{d!\left(\dfrac{(j+1)!}{(\gamma+\frac{1}{\alpha})}+\dfrac{j!}{\rho_k}\right)\left(\dfrac{i\gamma}{\rho_k(1-i\gamma)}\right)^{d-l}}{(d-l)!(x+1)^{l+1}}\right)$,

- $\Sigma^2_{i,j,d}(\gamma) = \sum_{l=0}^{d+1}\left(\dfrac{(d+1)!j!\left(\dfrac{i\gamma}{\rho_k(1-i\gamma)}\right)^{d+1-l}}{(d+1-l)!(\gamma+1)^{l+1}}\right)$,

- and $U(.)$ denotes the unit step function.

Indeed, when $\mathcal{H}_0$ is verified, the beam is attributed to a CU at random and the pdf of the SINR can be approximated by $p_0(\gamma)$.

Similarly, R_Q can be approximated by:

$$R_Q \simeq N_s\left(P_{\mathcal{H}_1}R_{Q\mathcal{H}_1}+P_{\mathcal{H}_0}R_{Q\mathcal{H}_0}\right), \tag{8}$$

where:

- $R_{Q\mathcal{H}_0}$ denotes the throughput of the secondary system with quantized feedback when hypothesis $\mathcal{H}_0$ occurs, and can be written as:

$$R_{Q\mathcal{H}_0} = \int_0^{+\infty}\log_2(1+\gamma)\,p_0(\gamma)\,d\gamma. \tag{9}$$

- $R_{Q\mathcal{H}_1}$ denotes the throughput of the secondary system with quantized feedback when hypothesis $\mathcal{H}_1$ occurs, and can be written as:

$$R_{Q\mathcal{H}_1} = \sum_{q=0}^{Q-1}\frac{\int_{b_q}^{b_{q+1}}\log_2(1+\gamma)\,p_0(\gamma)\,d\gamma}{\int_{b_q}^{b_{q+1}}p_0(\gamma)\,d\gamma}\int_{b_q}^{b_{q+1}}p_1(\gamma)\,d\gamma. \tag{10}$$

Then, after proper substitution, the loss in secondary system throughput due to the quantization is equal to:

$$R_{loss} = N_s P_{\mathcal{H}_1}\left(\int_0^{+\infty}\log_2(1+\gamma)\,p_2(\gamma)\,d\gamma\right.$$

$$\left.-\sum_{q=0}^{Q-1}\frac{\int_{b_q}^{b_{q+1}}\log_2(1+\gamma)\,p_0(\gamma)\,d\gamma}{\int_{b_q}^{b_{q+1}}p_0(\gamma)\,d\gamma}\int_{b_q}^{b_{q+1}}p_1(\gamma)\,d\gamma\right). \tag{11}$$

Minimizing the throughput loss R_{loss} is equivalent to maximizing $R_{Q\mathcal{H}_1}$, given in (10). Thus, we propose the following algorithm (Algorithm 1) to determine the optimal set of quantization thresholds.

Algorithm 1. Proposed algorithm

---

1. **Initialization:**
   - $b_0 = 0$,
   - $b_Q = 100$,
   - $\max R_{Q\mathcal{H}_1} = -\infty$
   - $\delta = 0.1$.

2. **Computation of the optimal decision levels:**
      for $b_1 = b_0 + \delta : \delta : b_Q$ **do**
         for $b_2 = b_1 + \delta : \delta : b_Q$ **do**
           $\vdots$

               for $b_{Q-1} = b_{Q-2} + \delta : \delta : b_Q$ **do**
                  Compute $R_{Q\mathcal{H}_1}$ using (10)
                  if $R_{Q\mathcal{H}_1} > \max R_{Q\mathcal{H}_1}$ **then**
                     $\max R_{Q\mathcal{H}_1} = R_{Q\mathcal{H}_1}$,

                     for $q = 1 : Q - 1$ **do**
                        $b_q^* = b_q$
                     end for
                  end if
               end for
           $\vdots$

         end for
      end for

---

4 Simulations Results

4.1 Comparison with the Pdf Matched Quantizer

In order to compare the performance of our proposed quantizer and the pdf matched quantizer proposed in [9], we plot in Fig. 2 the throughput of the cognitive system Vs the number of secondary users for $M = 4$, $1 \leq k \leq K$, $b \in \{2, 3\}$, $\rho = 5\,\mathrm{dB}$, $N_s = 3$. The Fig. 2 also shows the throughput obtained for the scheme proposed in [2] with full feed-back. In this figure, we compare the analytical result in (3) and (8) (shown in red) to the simulation result (shown in blue) for:

- our proposed quantizer
- the pdf matched quantizer
- and the case where full feed-back is adopted.

It is evident that the results attained by Matlab simulations match those attained by theoretical study. In addition, we notice that our proposed quantizer clearly outperforms the pdf matched quantizer and approaches the sum rate obtained with the full feed-back especially when the number of CU increases. We observe that the secondary system throughput raises with the full number of secondary users as well as with the number of quantization bits b. This can be explained by the increase of multi-user diversity [8]. Indeed, in [8] Sharif *et al.* showed that, in a Gaussian broadcast channel with M transmit antennas and K single antenna users, the sum rate capacity scales like $Mloglog(K)$ for large K.

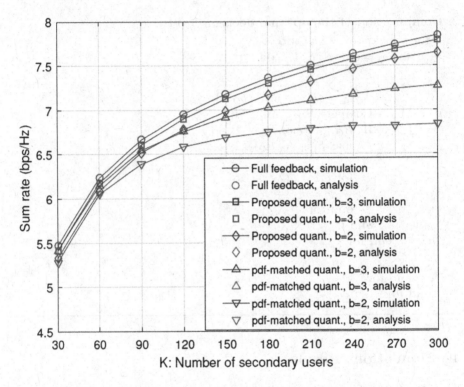

Fig. 2. Sum rate of the cognitive network Vs the number of CUs (the proposed quantizer and the pdf matched quantizer) for $\rho = 5\,dB$, $M = 4$, $N_s = 3$ and different values of b

The sum rate loss Vs the number of quantization bits b for $\rho = 5\,dB$, $M = 4$, $K = 300$ and $N_s = 3$ is shown in Fig. 3 for:

- our proposed algorithm,
- the pdf matched algorithm.

In this figure, we observe that the analytical curves are inline with the curves obtained by simulations for the tow algorithms. It is clear that our proposed algorithm outperforms the pdf matched algorithm in terms of sum rate loss. We notice also that our proposed quantizer converges much faster than the pdf matched quantizer to the one obtained with full feed-back as b increases. Indeed, when the number of quantization bits b increases, the quantization errors for maximizing the SINR decreases.

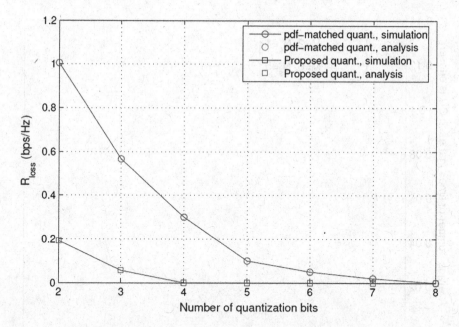

Fig. 3. Sum rate loss Vs the number of quantization bits b (the proposed quantizer and the pdf matched quantizer) for $M = 4$, $K = 300$, $\rho = 5\,$dB and $N_s = 3$

4.2 Fairness of the Proposed Scheduling Scheme

Now, in this part, we tackle the fairness of our proposed cognitive users scheduling. The fairness in scheduling algorithm means that the chance of choosing cognitive users with different SNRs is equal. In [8], authors demonstrated that the system based on opportunistic beam forming is fair when the number of beams increases more rapidly than (or equal to) $log(K)$. Consequently, cognitive network can achieve, simultaneously, fairness and maximum sum-rate. In the sequel, we study by Matlab simulations the equity of our new scheduling method. The average number of occasions that every CU is chosen Vs the SNR (ρ_k of the kth CU) is shown in Fig. 4 for $M \in \{2, 6\}$, $K = 50$ and $N_s \in \{1, 5\}$. The SNRs of cognitive users are distributed equally from $5\,$dB to $20\,$dB. As a result, the CUs associated to the SNR of 5 (resp. $20\,$dB) represent the lowest (resp. the greatest) CUs. We remark that, when $N_s = 1$ and $M = 2$ (shown in blue) the CU with the least SNR is seldom selected to be transmitted. We remark also that, when $N_s = 5$ and $M = 6$ (shown in red), the chance of selecting CUs with various SNRs is approximately equal since $N_s > log(K)$ as awaited, which demonstrates the equity of the designed scheme.

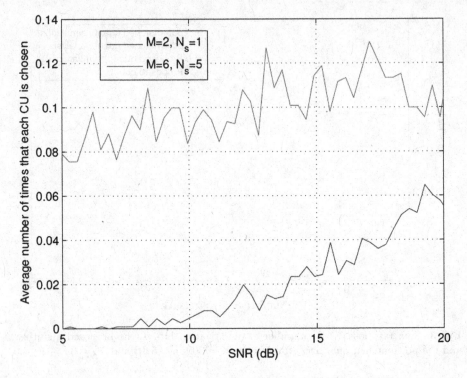

Fig. 4. Frequency of selecting each secondary user Vs SNR for different values of N_s and M and $K = 50$ (Color figure online)

5   Conclusions

This paper is concerned with scheduling for a cognitive radio network comprising multi-antenna secondary users (CUs) sharing the spectrum with a primary system. We proposed a new adaptive quantization scheme that minimizes the cognitive system sum-rate loss due to the SINR quantization. We compared the performances of our proposed algorithm with those of the pdf matched quantizer. In addition, we demonstrated via simulation that our proposed algorithm could achieve maximum throughput and fairness simultaneously.

References

1. Mitola, J., Maguire, G.Q.: Cognitive radio: making software radios more personal. IEEE Pers. Commun. **6**(4), 13–18 (1999). https://doi.org/10.1109/98.788210
2. Massaoudi, A., Sellami, N., Siala, M.: Scheduling scheme for cognitive radio networks with imperfect channel knowledge. In: PIMRC, pp. 3145–3149 (2013)
3. Massaoudi, A., Sellami, N., Siala, M.: A multi-threshold feedback scheme for cognitive radio networks based on opportunistic beamforming. In: The 22nd European Signal Processing Conference (EUSIPCO) (2014)

4. Massaoudi, A., Sellami, N., Siala, M.: Analysis of feedback multi thresholding in cognitive radio networks based on opportunistic beamforming. In: COMNET, pp. 1–5 (2015). https://doi.org/10.1109/COMNET.2015.7566618

5. Massaoudi, A., Sellami, N., Siala, M.: Cognitive radio networks based on opportunistic beamforming with quantized feedback. In: The 23rd European Signal Processing Conference (EUSIPCO) pp. 1217–1221 (2015). https://doi.org/10.1109/EUSIPCO.2015.7362577

6. Massaoudi, A., Sellami, N., Siala, M.: On the impact of pdf-matched quantization for heterogeneous cognitive radio networks. In: 2016 International Symposium on Signal, Image, Video and Communications (ISIVC), pp. 259–263 (2016). https://doi.org/10.1109/ISIVC.2016.7893997

7. Awoyemi, B.S., Maharaj, B.T.: Mitigating interference in the resource optimisation for heterogeneous cognitive radio networks. In: 2019 IEEE 2nd Wireless Africa Conference (WAC), pp. 1–6 (2019). https://doi.org/10.1109/AFRICA.2019.8843427

8. Sharif, M., Hassibi, B.: On the capacity of MIMO broadcast channels with partial side information. IEEE Trans. Inf. Theory 51, 506–522 (2005)

9. Anton-Haro, C.: On the impact of pdf-matched quantization on orthogonal random beamforming. IEEE Commun. Lett. 11(4), 328–330 (2007)

10. Yang, H.C., Lu, P., Sung, H.K., chai Ko, Y.: Exact sum-rate analysis of MIMO broadcast channels with random unitary beamforming based on quantized SINR feedback. In: ICC, pp. 3669–3673 (2008)

11. Ozdemir, O., Torlak, M.: Optimum feedback quantization in an opportunistic beamforming scheme. IEEE Trans. Wireless Commun. 9(5), 1584–1593 (2010)

12. Moon, S., Lee, S., Kim, J., Lee, I.: Channel quantization for block diagonalization with limited feedback in multiuser mimo downlink channels. J. Commun. Netw. 16(1), 1–9 (2014). https://doi.org/10.1109/JCN.2014.000003

13. Panda, A.V., Mishra, S.K., Dash, S.S., Bansal, N.: A suboptimal scheduling scheme for MIMO broadcast channels with quantized SINR. In: 2016 International Conference on Advances in Computing, Communications and Informatics (ICACCI), pp. 2175–2179 (2016). https://doi.org/10.1109/ICACCI.2016.7732374

14. Lloyd, S.: Least squares quantization in PCM. IEEE Trans. Inf. Theory 28(2), 129–137 (1982)

An Efficient Fault-Tolerant Scheduling Approach with Energy Minimization for Hard Real-Time Embedded Systems

Barkahoum Kada[(✉)] [iD] and Hamoudi Kalla

Batna2 University, 05000 Batna, Algeria
{b.kada, hamoudi.kalla}@univ-batna2.dz

Abstract. In this paper, we focus on two major problems in hard real-time embedded systems fault-tolerance and energy minimization. Fault-tolerance is achieved via both checkpointing technique and active replication strategy to tolerate multiple transient faults, whereas energy minimization is achieved by adapting Dynamic Voltage Frequency Scaling (DVFS) technique. First, we introduce an original fault-tolerance approach for hard real-time systems on multiprocessor platforms. Based on this approach, we then propose DVFS_FTS algorithm for energy-efficient fault-tolerant scheduling of precedence-constrained applications. DVFS_FTS is based on a list scheduling heuristics, it satisfies real-time constraints and minimizes energy consumption even in the presence of faults by exploring the multiprocessor architecture. The experimental results reveal that the proposed algorithm can reduce a considerable amount of energy while ensuring the required fault-tolerance of the system and outperforms other related approaches.

Keywords: Fault-tolerance · Checkpointing and active replication · Energy minimization

1 Introduction

Energy consumption and fault-tolerance have attracted a lot of interest in the design of modern embedded real-time systems. Fault-tolerance is fundamental for these systems to ensure their correct functionality and to meet their real-time constraints even in the occurrence of faults. Due to the high complexity, smaller transistors sizes, higher operational frequency, and lowering voltages [1–5], the number of faults is dramatically increasing, particularly the transient faults.

Power/energy management is an active area of research and many techniques have been proposed to minimize energy consumption under a large diversity of system and task models [6, 7]. Dynamic voltage and frequency scaling (DVFS) is an energy saving technique enabled on most of the modern processors. It enables a processor to operate at multiple voltages where each corresponds to a specific frequency [8].

This paper attempts to solve the following problem "Given a set Γ of hard real-time dependent tasks and a set $\mathcal{P}$ of homogeneous processors which support L frequency

© Springer Nature Switzerland AG 2020
I. Jemili and M. Mosbah (Eds.): DiCES-N 2019, CCIS 1130, pp. 102–117, 2020.
https://doi.org/10.1007/978-3-030-40131-3_7

levels, find the scheduling for all tasks in Γ such that the total energy consumption is reduced without any deadline miss while ensuring fault-tolerance requirement".

The following contributions are presented in this work:

- An original fault-tolerance strategy is proposed to tolerate k transient faults with the guarantee of deadline constraints. This strategy combines checkpointing and active replication to efficiently explore the architecture and application time-constraints.
- To our knowledge, we are the first introducing collaboration between the primary and the backup replicas of the same task in case of active replication to tolerate temporally or spatially faults.
- Extending the proposed fault-tolerance strategy to incorporate it with DVFS technique to achieve more energy saving.
- An efficient fault-tolerant scheduling heuristic DVFS_FTS of precedence-constrained applications based on the earliest-deadline-first (EDF) algorithm and the proposed fault-tolerance strategy is presented to minimize the system energy consumption while tolerating k transient faults.

The rest of this paper is organized as follows. An overview of related work is provided in Sect. 2. The system models considered in this work are introduced in Sect. 3. The proposed fault-tolerance approach is explained in Sect. 4. The strategy that utilizes this approach and DVFS technique to minimize energy is provided in Sect. 5. The proposed DVFS_FTS algorithm is presented in Sect. 6. Simulation results are discussed in Sect. 7. Finally, the conclusion is given in Sect. 8.

2   Related Work

Several papers have been published are closely related to our research, these researches differ in many aspects, such as task models (dependent or independent tasks, hard or soft deadlines, periodic or aperiodic tasks), multiprocessor or uniprocessor platforms, online or offline scheduling and the fault-tolerance technique adopted.

The authors in [9] proposed a tri-criteria scheduling algorithm for minimizing the makespan, the energy consumption and maximizing the system reliability. As fault-tolerance technique, they used active replication of tasks and data dependencies. For energy minimization, they used dynamic voltage scaling DVS.

The primary-backup (passive replication) approach is used by Samal et al. [10] as a fault-tolerant scheduling technique to ensure timing constraints when permanent or transient fault occurs. Gan et al. [11] proposed a synthesis approach to decide the mapping of hard real-time applications on distributed heterogeneous systems, such that multiple transient faults are tolerated, and the energy consumed is minimized. For recovery from faults, they used replication technique.

Software replication techniques are more useful to tackle permanent faults and are preferred for safety-critical applications but they imposed significant cost constraints.

Checkpointing with rollback recovery [7, 12–15] and re-execution [16] are referenced in [17] as time based redundancy techniques. These techniques recover from transient faults by consecutive executions on the processor executing the faulty task.

Djosic and Jevtic [1] developed a fault-tolerant DVFS algorithm for real-time application of independent tasks. This algorithm combines DVFS for optimizing energy consumption and re-execution recovery for fault-tolerance, but their scope is restricted to single processor systems. Han *et al.* [18] introduced an effective strategy to determine the checkpointing state that can tolerate a fixed number of faults on uniprocessor architecture. Also, they proposed a task allocation scheme to reduce energy consumption.

Few papers related to our work [19, 20] have combined replication and time-based redundancy methods to tolerate multiple faults with low cost in terms of energy consumption and execution time. For example, Pop *et al.* [19] have proposed a synthesis approach that decides the assignment of fault-tolerance technique to each task in the application, for instance checkpointing, active replication or their combination. However, energy consumption is not studied in their proposition. An online task scheduling for energy minimization and high reliability have been proposed by Tavana *et al.* [20]. For fault-tolerance, They applied on priority hardware-redundancy and second re-execution. For power management, they used two techniques: DPM (Dynamic Power Management) on the spare unit and DVS (Dynamic Voltage Scaling) on the primary processor.

3 System Models

3.1 Application Model

In this work, we consider real-time applications with n hard aperiodic dependent tasks $\Gamma = \{\tau_1, \tau_2, \ldots, \tau_n\}$ which can be modeled by a directed acyclic graph (DAG). Tasks are non-preemptive and cannot be interrupted by other tasks. Tasks send their output values in messages, when terminated. All required inputs have to arrive before activation of the task. The dependence $\tau_i \rightarrow \tau_j$ means that τ_i execution precedes τ_j execution. Figure 1 shows an example of DAG G_1 with 5 nodes which models an application $A_1 = \{\tau_1, \tau_2, \ldots, \tau_5\}$. The worst case execution time for the task τ_i at the maximum frequency/voltage in a fault free condition is denoted C_i and D_i is the deadline of the task. The utilization of task τ_i is defined in Eq. 1:

$$U_i = \frac{C_i}{D_i} \qquad \text{where } 0 \leq U_i \leq 1 \tag{1}$$

The system utilization is therefore calculated according to Eq. 2:

$$U = \sum_{i=1}^{n} U_i \tag{2}$$

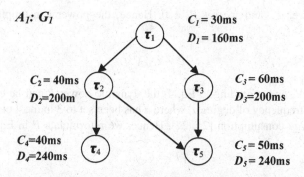

Fig. 1. Hard real-time application example.

3.2 Fault Model

During the execution of an application, faults may be hard to avoid due to different reasons, such as hardware failure, software errors, devices exposed to intense temperatures, and external impacts [21]. As a result, transient faults are more frequent than permanent ones. Hence, the authors in this paper are interested in tolerating transient faults as their number has been dramatically higher.

3.3 Architecture and Energy Model

We consider architecture composed of a set of m homogeneous processors $\mathbb{P} = \{P_1, P_2, ..., P_m\}$. Each processor $P_i \in \mathbb{P}$ is connected with the others through point-to-point communication links and is DVFS enabled with a set of L operating frequencies. We denoted with $F = \{f_1, f_2, ..., f_L\}$ with $0 \leq f_L \leq f_{L-1} \leq \cdots \leq f_1 = f_{max}$. We assume the frequency values are normalized with respect to f_{max}, i.e. $f_{max} = 1$.

The energy model used in this work is the same to the one used in the literature [1, 6, 9] and [21], where the power consumption P of a system is given by Eq. 3:

$$P = P_S + h(P_{ind} + P_d) = P_S + h(P_{ind} + C_{ef}V^2 f) \tag{3}$$

Where P_S is the static power, P_{ind} is the frequency-independent power and P_d is the frequency-dependent power. The parameter $h = 1$ when the system is in the working state. Otherwise, when the system is in the standby state, $h = 0$. C_{ef} is the effective loading capacitance and V is the supply voltage and it is a function of working frequency f. The static power can be removed only by turning off the whole system, P_{ind} is a constant independent of operating frequency. As the energy consumption due to frequency scaling is independent of P_S, we take into account only the frequency-dependent power P_d and we set $P_S = 0$. Hence, the power consumption P can be written as:

$$P = C_{ef} V^2 f \tag{4}$$

Since $f \propto V$, and according to Eq. 4, the dynamic power P can be expressed as a polynomial of frequency of degree α, where α has been set to 3 in most of the published papers on energy consumption [21, 22]. Hence, we reformulate P in Eq. 5 as:

$$P = C_{ef} f^3 \tag{5}$$

The energy consumed by task τ_i is given by Eq. 6:

$$E_i(f_i) = C_{ef} C_i f_i^2 \tag{6}$$

Where C_i is the execution time of task τ_i under frequency f_i. The total energy E_{total} consumed by processors during the execution of a task set is expressed by Eq. 7:

$$E_{total} = \sum_{i=1}^{n} E_i(f_i) \tag{7}$$

In this study, we consider only processor energy consumption.

4 Fault-Tolerance Strategy

Our fault-tolerance strategy combines the two well-known techniques for tolerating faults: uniform checkpointing with rollback recovery and active replication. These two techniques guarantee during the application's execution, the satisfaction of timing constraints and provide high reliability even in the presence of faults.

When applying uniform checkpointing with rollbacks, the application rolls back to the last saved checkpoint and re-execute the faulty interval [19]. Inserting one checkpoint to task τ_i refers to save its current state in memory for recovery. Active replication is used in the case that checkpointing with rollbacks can not satisfy task deadline.

4.1 Uniform Checkpointing

Uniform checkpointing with rollback recovery reduces re-execution time of the faulty task. Inserting uniform checkpoints means that the task is devided into uniform checkpoint intervals. In case of fault detection, the last saved checkpoint will be restored to re-execute the faulty interval [19].

The execution time of task τ_i with m_i checkpoints in the fault-free condition is given as Eq. 8

$$C_i(m_i) = C_i + m_i O_i \tag{8}$$

The recovery time of τ_i with m_i checkpoints under a single failure is formulated in Eq. 9

$$R_i(m_i) = r_i + \frac{C_i}{m_i} \qquad (9)$$

Where O_i and r_i represent respectively the time overheads for saving one checkpoint and recovering from checkpoint.

The worst-case response time $WCRT_i$ of task τ_i using uniform checkpointing with rollback recovery and assuming k faults is given by Eq. 10:

$$WCRT_i(m_i) = C_i(m_i) + k * R_i(m_i) \qquad (10)$$

It is proofed by Pop *et al.* [19] that the optimal number of checkpoints m_i^* to minimize the worst-case response time $WCRT_i$ in the presence of k faults can be calculated as:

$$m_i^* = \left\| \sqrt{\frac{k * C_i}{O_i}} \right\| \qquad (11)$$

We give an example of uniform checkpointing in Fig. 2. The task τ_1 with worst execution time $C_1 = 60$ ms (Fig. 2.a) is checkpointed with two equidistant checkpoints which result two equal intervals $\tau_{1(1)}$ and $\tau_{1(2)}$ (Fig. 2.b). In Fig. 2.c, a fault affects the second interval $\tau_{1(2)}$. This faulty interval is re-executed again starting from the second checkpoint.

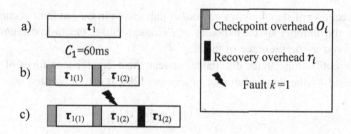

Fig. 2. Uniform checkpointing with rollback recovery.

4.2   Collaborative Active Replication

Uniform checkpointing with rollback recovery technique cannot explore the available processors in the architecture to reduce the schedule length [23]. If the task experiences a fault, then it has to recover on the same processor. In contrast, software replication techniques (active and passive replication) can utilize the spare capacity of the other processors. With active replication, all the task replicas are executed independent of fault occurrences [24]. However, with passive replication, backup replicas are executed only if the primary replica is faulty.

In this research, we use active replication in case that checkpointing with rollbacks cannot satisfy task τ_i deadline. The task τ_i is replicated on two collaborative replicas; τ_i^1 and τ_i^2, both of which are assigned on different processors [29].

For the sake of uniformity and clarity, we will consider the original task τ_i as the primary replica τ_i^1 and its replica as the backup replica τ_i^2. We make the following suppositions:

- The checkpoint saving and rollback recovery are themselves fault-tolerant.
- The primary replica τ_i^1 and the backup one τ_i^2 cannot be faulty simultaneously.
- Faults are detected as soon as they occur, and the recovery will be with the no faulty replica.

Due to multiple fault occurrence, both primary and backup replicas may be faulty. Therefore, active replication alone will be infeasible as in [17]. Thus, to achieve the feasibility of our strategy, collaboration between replicas is introduced to tolerate each coming fault in the primary or the backup replicas (τ_i^1, τ_i^2).

For calculation reasons, we use an additional processor $P\#$. The proposed approach is performed according to the following steps:

Step1: τ_i is scheduled on the processor $P\#$ ($\tau_i\#$) as illustrated in Fig. 3a;
Step2: $\tau_i\#$ is checkpointed with the appropriate m_i^* checkpoints obtained with Eq. 11;
Step3: τ_i is replicated, which will result in two replicas τ_i^1 and τ_i^2, both of which must be scheduled on two processors;
Step 4: The initial checkpoints of the task $\tau_i\#$ are projected onto τ_i^1 and τ_i^2 alternatively, as illustrated in Fig. 3b.

The execution of step 4 allows replicas collaboration in case of fault occurrence and minimizes the number of checkpoints m_i^*. Consequently, the task deadline can be respected even in the presence of faults.

Δ represents in Fig. 3b the difference between the execution start times of τ_i^1 and τ_i^2, which depend on the disponibility of processors [29]. It can be written as:

$$\Delta = ST\left(\tau_i^1\right) - ST\left(\tau_i^2\right) \tag{12}$$

To ensure the success of step 4, Δ should verify the following:

$$0 \leq \Delta \leq \frac{C_i}{m_i} \tag{13}$$

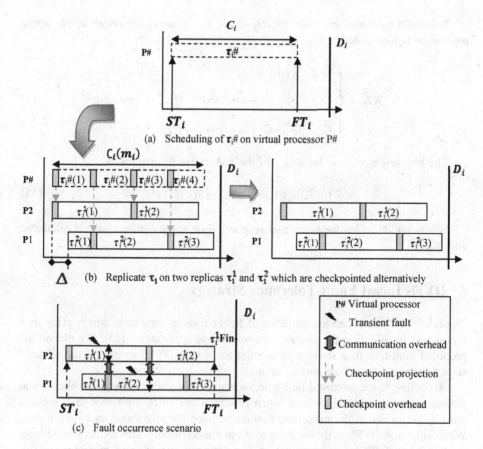

(a) Scheduling of $\tau_i\#$ on virtual processor P#

(b) Replicate τ_1 on two replicas τ_1^1 and τ_1^2 which are checkpointed alternatively

(c) Fault occurrence scenario

Fig. 3. Illustration of different steps of collaborative active replication.

If one of the replicas(τ_i^1 or τ_i^2) is faulty, the state of the successful replica will be transmitted to the faulty one at checkpoint with Send/Receive communication to continue the execution. As shown in Fig. 3c, when fault affects the first execution interval $\tau_i^1(1)$, the no faulty replica τ_i^2 sends at checkpoint the correct state to the faulty task via communication step.

With alternative checkpointing scheme, the number of checkpoints in each replica is equal to $\lfloor \frac{m_i}{2} \rfloor$ or $\lceil \frac{m_i}{2} \rceil$. Hence, in the fault free condition ($k = 0$), the worst case response time $WCRT_i$ of the task τ_i is given by the term ($C_i + \lfloor \frac{m_i}{2} \rfloor * O_i$). Where O_i is the time overhead for saving one checkpoint.

In case of fault occurrence, the recovery from fault is provided with communication step between the replicas τ_i^1 and τ_i^2. We denote the communication overhead by $com(\tau_i^1, \tau_i^2)$.

The worst case response time $WCRT_i$ of the task τ_i using the collaborative active replication is formulated in Eq. 14:

$$WCRT_i = \begin{cases} C_i + \lfloor \frac{m_i}{2} \rfloor * O_i, & if\ k = 0 \\ C_i + \lceil \frac{m_i}{2} \rceil * O_i + k * com(\tau_i^1, \tau_i^2) & otherwise\ or \\ C_i + \lfloor \frac{m_i}{2} \rfloor * O_i + k * com(\tau_i^1, \tau_i^2) \end{cases} \quad (14)$$

The best response time $WCRT_{best}$ of the task τ_i can be written as:

$$WCRT_{best}(\tau_i) = \min_{1 \le j \le 2} WCRT(\tau_i^j) \quad (15)$$

Where $WCRT(\tau_i^j)$ is the worst case response time of the replica τ_i^j and is calculated with Eq. 14.

5   DVFS Based Fault-Tolerance Strategy

The DVFS technique can assign different frequencies to each task, which gives us a useful way to minimize the energy consumption of applications [25]. We extend the proposed fault-tolerance strategy to incorporate it with DVFS to exploit the released slack time to achieve more energy saving.

According to the proposed fault-tolerance approach, we adopt active replication to guarantee timing constraints even when deadlines are strict. However, task replicas must be performed at the maximum frequency given the probability of failure is low. We assume that DVFS is used during uniform checkpointing with rollback technique.

Similar to [18], we assume that checkpointing is not affected by processor frequency. We focus on the fault-free execution and like [2] and [26], we aim to reduce the fault-free energy consumption because recovery executions have a small probability of being performed, and for this reason their energy consumption is a negligible fraction of the total energy consumption. The recovery time of a faulty task is always performed at the maximum frequency to preserve its original reliability.

In the next,, we search the optimal frequency assignments assuming all tasks their deadlines. In the existence of precedence constraints, a task may have to complete well before its deadline to ensure that all its successor tasks can finish in time. We can redefine the effective deadline of a task τ_i as in [27] as follows:

$$D_i^{ef} = \begin{cases} D_i & ,succ(\tau_i) = \emptyset \\ min(D_i, D_j^{ef} - C_j) & ,\tau_j \in succ(\tau_i) \end{cases} \quad (16)$$

Where $succ(\tau_i)$ is the set of successor tasks of τ_i.

The frequency f_i^{opt} that allows task τ_i to successfully complete execution before its deadline D_i^{ef} while minimizing energy consumption and tolerating k faults with checkpointing with rollback should satisfy the following:

$$ST_i + \frac{C_i(m_i)}{f_i^{opt}} + k * R_i(m_i) \leq D_i^{ef} \qquad (17)$$

Where ST_i and $\frac{C_i(m_i)}{f_i^{opt}}$ are respectively the start time and the fault-free execution time of task τ_i with m_i checkpoints performed at frequency f_i^{opt}. $R_i(m_i)$ is the recovery time of τ_i under a single failure performed at the maximum frequency f_{max} ($C_i(m_i)$ and $R(m_i)$ were defined with Eqs. 7 and 8 respectively).

After evaluation of Eq. 20, we obtain the following solution:

$$f_i^{opt} \geq \frac{C_i(m_i)}{D_i^{ef} - ST_i - k * R_i(m_i)} \qquad (18)$$

If $f_i^{opt} \nexists F$, we choose neighboring frequencies $f_L < f_i^{opt} < f_{L-1}$ and $f_{L-1}, f_L \in F$. Hence, the minimize energy consumed during the execution of task τ_i is given by:

$$E_i\left(f_i^{opt}\right) = C_{ef} \frac{C_i(m_i)}{f_i^{opt}} f_i^{opt^2} = C_{ef} C_i(m_i) f_i^{opt} = C_{ef} \frac{C_i(m_i)^2}{D_i^{ef} - ST_i - k * R_i(m_i)} \qquad (19)$$

6 The Proposed DVFS_ FTS Algorithm

Figure 4 presents the proposed DVFS fault-tolerant scheduling algorithm. This algorithm takes as input the application A, the number k of transient faults that have to be tolerated, the architecture P, the set of frequency levels F and timing constraints.

Our algorithm uses the notion of ready task that means that all task predecessors have been scheduled. First, the list TReady is initialized with tasks without predecessors (line 1). Then, while TReady isn't empty (line 4), we place in the schedule the ready task τ_i with minimum deadline (line 5). After, the maximum response time of the task τ_i will be calculated with Eq. 10 under maximum frequency (line 6). The checkpointing with rollback policy will be applied if the task deadline can be satisfied on the processor P_j at the earliest start time (line 10–13). In this case, the task τ_i will be performed under the frequency f_i^{opt} calculated based on Eq. 21 (line 12–13). Otherwise, the task τ_i will be replicated on two replicas (τ_i^1 and τ_i^2) and its maximum response time will be calculated with Eq. 14 under the maximum frequency (line 14–18). After execution of the task τ_i, its energy consumption will be calculated and the total energy will be updated in lines 22–23. Finally, the task τ_i will be deleted from the list TReady and all its successors are added to the list in line 24.

DVFS_FTS Algorithm

Inputs:

$\Gamma = \{\tau_1, \tau_2, \dots \tau_n\}$

$\mathcal{P} = \{P_1, P_2, \dots, P_m\}$

$F = \{f_1, f_2, \dots, f_l\}$

K transient faults for each task

Real-time constraints

1. TReady = $\{\tau_i \in \Gamma \mid pred(t_i) = \emptyset\}$
2. Schedulable = True
3. $E_{total} = 0$
4. While $TReady \neq \emptyset$ do
5. { Select $\tau_i \in TReady$ having the minimum deadline D_i
6.   compute $WCRT_i$ with Equation 10 under maximum frequency
7.   compute the start time ST_{ij} of τ_i on all processor P_j in $\mathcal{P}$
8. $ST_i = min_{j=1..m} ST_{ij}$
9.   If $D_i - ST_i \geq WCRT_i$ then
10.   { Schedule τ_i on P_j at the earliest start time   /* P_j is the processor with min ST_i*/
11.   Apply checkpointing for τ_i
12.   compute f_i^{opt} based on Equation 18
13.   Perform τ_i under f_i^{opt} frequency }
14.   Else
15.   { compute $WCRT_i$ with Equation 14 under maximum frequency
16.   If $D_i - ST_i \geq WCRT_i$ then
17.   { Schedule both τ_i on P_j and its replica on another processor P_k at the earliest start time.
18.   Apply collaborative active replication for τ_i }
19.   Else
20.   { Schedulable = False
21.   break }}
22. compute the energy consumption $E_i(f_i)$
23. $E_{total} = E_{total} + E_i(f_i)$
24. TReady = TReady- $\{\tau_i\} \cup \{\tau_j \in succ(\tau_i)\mid pred(\tau_j) ∄ TReady\}$
25. }End DVFS_FTS

Fig. 4. The proposed DVFS_FTS algorithm.

7 · Performance Evaluation

In this section, we evaluate the performance of our algorithm DVFS_FTS in term of energy saving. For comparison, we have implemented our algorithm and the following schemes:

EXH_FTS: Fault-tolerant scheduling algorithm with energy minimization using exhaustion method.

DVFS_CH: Fault-tolerant scheduling algorithm that uses checkpointing with roll back technique for fault-tolerance and DVS for reduce energy. This algorithm is extended from JFTT scheme [15] for tasks with precedence constraints (application DAG).

We choose the **EXH_FTS** algorithm as the exhaustion method is widely used in the literature [1, 18] to search the optimal frequency assignment for which the energy consumption is minimal. With **DVFS_CH**, we evaluate the effect of the proposed fault-tolerance strategy in energy saving compared with the one that is used extensively in research work: the checkpointing technique.

The energy saving *ES* can be calculated as Eq. 20.

$$ES = 100 * \frac{E_{FTS} - E}{E_{FTS}} \tag{20}$$

Where E_{FTS} represents the energy consumption of the proposed algorithm with all tasks are executed at the highest frequency and E is the energy consumption of a compared algorithm.

7.1 Simulation Parameters

Table 1 summarizes the simulation parameters of our experiments which are the followings: The method of generating random graphs is the same as [28]. We have generated a set of DAG applications with 10, 20, 30, 40 and 50 tasks. Within a task set, the worst-case execution time on maximum operating frequency C_i for each task is randomly generated with values uniformly distributed in the range of [10 ms, 100 ms]. We assume $C_{ef} = 1$ and the operating frequencies are set as $F = \{0.1, 0.2, \ldots, 1\}$.

Table 1. Parameters for simulation

Parameter	Value(fixed-varied)
Number of processors	4
Application size (Number of tasks)	(10, 20, 30, 40, 50)
Execution time (ms)	[10, 100]
Normalized frequency	[0.1–1] with a step of 0.1
Checkpoint overhead O	(1%, 2%, 5%, 10%, 15%, 20%)
Number of faults k	(1, 2, 3, 4, 5)

7.2 Experiment Results

Figure 5 shows the effect of increasing the number of transient faults on energy savings of the three algorithms. In this experiments, we set application size $\Gamma = 10$ tasks, the checkpoint overhead $O = 2\%$ and vary k from 1 to 5. As can be seen clearly from the figure that the performance on energy saving of DVFS_FTS algorithm outperforms both DVFS_CH and EXH_FTS schemes. For instance, when the number of transient faults is 5 faults, the *ES* of DVFS_FTS is greater than DVFS_CH and EXH_FTS by

7.17% and 6.34% respectively. Furthermore, we can see that the energy savings of these algorithms decrease with the increase of the number of transient faults.

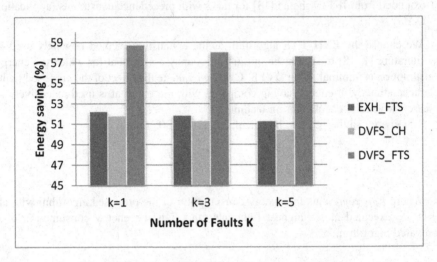

Fig. 5. The impact of number of faults on energy saving.

The second set of experiments is to investigate the performance of the different approaches with respect to application size (see Fig. 6). In this set of experiments, we set the checkpoint overhead $O = 2\%$ and $k = 3$ and vary the application size Γ from 10 tasks to 50 tasks. We can see that the energy saving increases when the number of tasks increases. The energy saving of DVFS_FTS is greater than DVFS_CH and EXH_FTS schemes by: (6.73%, 6.18%), (6.76%, 5.8%), (7.68%, 6.75%), (8.74%, 8.45%), (8.61%, 8.8%) for number of tasks of 10, 20, 30, 40 and 50, respectively. We can resume that our algorithm performs better than the other algorithms.

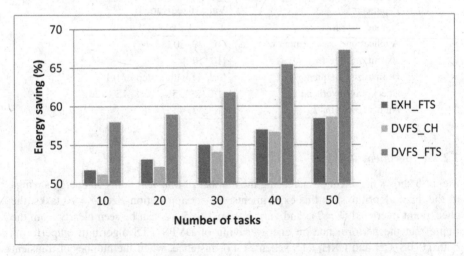

Fig. 6. The impact of application size on energy saving considering k = 3 faults.

In the third set of experiments, we show the impact of checkpointing overhead on the performance of algorithms (see Fig. 7). In this set of experiments, we set application size $\Gamma = 20$ tasks, $k = 3$ faults and vary O from 1% to 20%. As can be seen from the figure, the energy saving of the three schemes decreases when O increases. However, the *ES* of DVFS_FTS decreases about 5.87% when O increases from 1% to 20% and less than the *ES* of DVFS_CH and EXH_FTS decrease about 6.5% and 6.76% respectively. Also, we can see that DVFS_CH and EXH_FTS give approximately the same response.

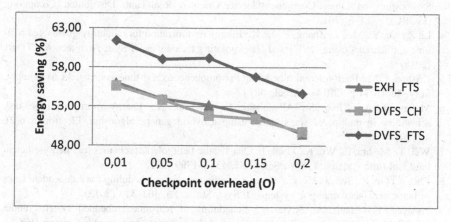

Fig. 7. The impact of checkpoint overhead on energy saving considering k = 3 faults.

From these experiments, we can resume that the proposed algorithm DVFS_FTS outperforms the other two algorithms.

8 Conclusion

In this paper, we have studied the trade-off between fault tolerance and energy minimization in hard real-time systems running on multiprocessor platforms. We first propose an efficient fault-tolerance approach that combines uniform checkpointing with rollback policy and collaborative active replication to explore hardware resources and timing constraint. We then present our fault-tolerant scheduling algorithm DVFS_FTS that exploits DVFS technology to reduce energy consumption and the proposed fault-tolerance approach to tolerating K transient faults for applications that can be modeled with a DAG (precedence-constrained applications). Simulation results have shown that the proposed algorithm achieves a considerable amount of energy saving compared to EXH_FTS and DVFS_CH algorithms.

Our work remains opening to future contributions like extend the proposed algorithm to heterogeneous multiprocessor platforms and improve the proposed collaborative active replication to achieve more energy saving. Furthermore, we will study another checkpointing strategy to minimize the optimal number of checkpoints for reducing scheduling length and energy consumption.

References

1. Djosic, S., Jevtic, M.: Dynamic voltage and frequency scaling algorithm for fault tolerant real-time systems. Microelectron. Reliab. J. **53**, 1036–1042 (2013)
2. Salehi, M., Tavana, M.K., Rehman, S., Shafique, M., Henkel, J.: Two-state checkpointing for energy-efficient fault tolerance in hard real-time systems. IEEE Trans. Very Large Scale Integr. (VLSI) Syst. **24**, 2426–2437 (2016)
3. Li, Z., Wang, L., Ren, S., Quan, G.: Energy minimization for checkpointing-based approach to guaranteeing real-time systems reliability. In: Proceedings of IEEE 16th International Symposium on Object/Component/Service-Oriented Real-Time Distributed Computing (ISORC), pp. 1–8 (2013)
4. Li, Z., Xu, Y., Mei, J., Zhang, F., Li, K.: Energy minimization for reliability-guaranteed real-time applications using DVFS and checkpointing techniques. J. Syst. Architect. **61**, 71–81 (2015)
5. Krishna, C.M.: Fault-tolerant scheduling in homogeneous real-time systems. ACM Comput. Surv. **46**(4), 34 p. (2014). (Article 48)
6. Mahmood, A., Khan, S., Albalooshi, F., Awwad, N.: Energy-aware real-time task scheduling in multiprocessor systems using a hybrid genetic algorithm. Electronics **6**(2), 40 (2017)
7. Wei, T., Mishra, P., Wu, K., Zhou, J.: Quasi-static fault tolerant schemes for energy-efficient hard real-time systems. J. Syst. Softw. **85**, 1386–1399 (2012)
8. Zhu, X., Ge, R., Sun, J., He, C.: 3E: energy-efficient elastic scheduling for independent tasks in heterogeneous computing systems. J. Syst. Softw. **86**, 302–314 (2013)
9. Assayad, I., Girault, A., Kalla, H.: Scheduling of real-time embedded systems under reliability and power constraints. In: International Conference on Complex Systems (ICCS). IEEE (2012)
10. Samal, A.K., Mall, R., Tripathy, C.: Fault tolerant scheduling of hard real-time tasks on multiprocessor system using a hybrid genetic algorithm. Swarm Evol. Comput. **14**, 92–105 (2014)
11. Gan, J., Gruian, F., Pop, P., Madsen, J.: Energy/reliability trade-offs in fault-tolerant event-triggered distributed embedded systems. In: Proceedings of the 16th Asia South Pacific Design Automation Conference (ASP-DAC), pp. 731–736 (2011)
12. Kumar, A., Alam, B.: Improved EDF algorithm for fault tolerance with energy minimization. In: IEEE International Conference on Computational Intelligence & Communication Technology (CICT), Ghaziabad, India (2015)
13. Han, Q., Quan, G., Fan, M.: Energy minimization for fault tolerant real-time applications on multiprocessor platforms scheduling using checkpointing. In: IEEE International Symposium on Low Power Electronics and Design (ISLPED), Beijing, China, pp. 76–81 (2013)
14. Izosimov, V., Pop, P., Eles, P., Peng, Z.: Scheduling and optimization of fault-tolerant embedded systems with transparency/performance trade-offs. ACM Trans. Embed. Comput. Syst. **11**(3), 61 (2012)
15. Zhang, Y., Chakrabarty, K.: A unified approach for fault tolerance and dynamic power management in fixed-priority real-time embedded systems. IEEE Trans. Comput.-Aided Des. Integr. Circuits Syst. **25**, 111–125 (2006)
16. Izosimov, V., Pop, P., Eles, P., Peng, Z.: Scheduling of fault tolerant embedded systems with soft and hard timing constraints. In: Proceedings of 2008 Design, Automation and Test in Europe Conference (DATE), pp. 915–920 (2008)
17. Motaghi, M.H., Zarandi, H.R.: DFTS: dynamic fault-tolerant scheduling for real-time tasks in multicore processors. Microprocess. Microsyst. J. **38**, 88–97 (2014)

18. Han, Q., Fan, M., Niu, L., Quan, G.: Energy minimization for fault tolerant scheduling of periodic fixed-priority applications on multiprocessor platforms. In: Proceedings of 2015 Design, Automation and Test in Europe Conference and Exhibition (DATE), pp. 830–835 (2015)
19. Izosimov, V., Pop, P., Eles, P., Peng, Z.: Design optimization of time-and- cost-constrained fault-tolerant embedded systems with checkpointing and replication. IEEE Trans. Very Large Scale Integr. Syst. **17**, 340–389 (2009)
20. Tavana, M.K., Teimouri, N., Abollahi, M., Goudarzi, M.: Simultaneous hardware and time redundancy with online task scheduling for low energy highly reliable standby-sparing system. ACM Trans. Embed. Comput. Syst. **13**(4), 86 (2014)
21. Zhang, L., Li, K., Xu, Y., Mei, J., Zhang, F., Li, K.: Maximizing reliability with energy conservation for parallel task scheduling in a heterogeneous cluster. Inf. Sci. **319**, 113–131 (2015)
22. Zahaf, H.E.: Energy efficient scheduling of parallel real-time tasks on heterogeneous multicore systems. Ph.D. Université de Lille 1, Sciences et Technologies (2016)
23. Eles, P., Izosimov, V., Pop, P., Peng, Z., et al.: Synthesis of fault-tolerant embedded systems. In: Proceedings of 2008 Design, Automation and Test in Europe Conference (DATE), pp. 1117–1122 (2008)
24. Girault, A., Kalla, H.: A novel bicriteria scheduling heuristics providing a guaranteed global system failure rate. IEEE Trans. Dependable Secure Comput. **6**, 241–254 (2009)
25. Hu, Y., Liu, C., Li, K., Chen, X., Li, K.: Slack allocation algorithm for energy minimization in cluster systems. Future Gener. Comput. Syst. **74**, 119–131 (2016)
26. Melhem, R., Mosse, D., Elnozahy, E.: The interplay of power management and fault recovery in real-time systems. IEEE Trans. Comput. **53**, 217–231 (2004)
27. Zhao, B., Ayden, H., Zhu, D.: Shared recovery for energy efficiency and reliability enhancements in real-time applications with precedence constraints. ACM Trans. Des. Autom. Electron. Syst., **18**(2) (2013). (Article 23)
28. Qamhieh, M.: Scheduling of parallel real-time DAG tasks on multiprocessor systems. Ph.D., Paris-Est University (2015)
29. Kada, B., Kalla, H.: A fault-tolerant scheduling algorithm based on checkpointing and redundancy for distributed real-time systems. Int. J. Distrib. Syst. Technol. **10**(3), 58–75 (2019)

Artificial Intelligence Applied to Cyber Physical Systems

Using Dynamic Bayesian Networks to Solve Road Traffic Congestion in the Sfax City

Ahmed Derbel[✉] and Younes Boujelbene[✉]

FSEG of Sfax, Sfax University, 3018 Sfax, Tunisia
derbelamd@gmail.com, boujelbene.younes@yahoo.fr

Abstract. The development of a road traffic management system is used to model traffic movements in the city and to detect road axes that are often congested. In this case, it will be important to measure the demand for travel and to simulate its contribution to urban congestion in Sfax city. With a view to improving traffic management, our contribution focuses on the adaptation of a method capable of both identifying the different relevant variables of road traffic, modeling the probabilistic dependence structure on a road segment and to analyze the probabilities of urban congestion. The results produced by the diagnosis and analysis provided elements of response to the questioning of road traffic management. We found that the city of Sfax has shown a failure in intra-urban transport services and the transport system in this region is not able to handle the expected increase in the volume of road traffic. We have demonstrated that the integration of public transport services contributes will improve traffic fluidity, and it is still able to make the public and urban space less polluting, more fluid and more attractive.

Keywords: Macroscopic traffic flow model · Bayesian network · Measuring road congestion · Sfax city

1 Introduction

The city of Sfax located in northern Africa in Tunisia continues to face considerable mobility and transportation challenges. This is due to a growing fleet of passengers and goods transporting through the city center, which is already contributing to pollution, congestion and a slowdown in road traffic. The city also suffers from poorly developed and poorly maintained road infrastructure and inadequate management of the transport system. In fact, like many around the world, Sfax is affected by environmental problems due to undisputed and undeniable pollution (CO_2 emissions, noise, vibration, visual impacts) and other identified road safety problem areas.

Despite its significant economic weight (2nd city and economic center of the country after Grand-Tunis), Sfax is a limited and constrained space where there is a relative scarcity of parking spaces, especially in its central space. All of factors are leading to rapidly rising car ownership and car use, and have become the main factors for a modal transfer away from public transport towards private car. This disadvantage is constantly exacerbated by the continuous increase in the number of vehicles in circulation. The rise of bank lending added to ease the acquisition of the ordinary

I. Jemili and M. Mosbah (Eds.): DiCES-N 2019, CCIS 1130, pp. 121–132, 2020.
https://doi.org/10.1007/978-3-030-40131-3_8

family car and has led to a considerable increase in the number of passenger cars in recent years. Sfax provides 38% of urban travel and that the Governorate currently has around 100000 vehicles, the number expected to reach 200000 units in 2020, only in Grand Sfax. To measure the road traffic situation in the city of Sfax, we propose an application of urban traffic management, with focus on identifying the main causes of congestion. The objective of our research is to examine the risk of congestion in the coming years and predict what the traffic situation in the future will be. This approach has been put in place to evaluate road traffic and to develop simulation scenarios based on a practical case adapted in the city of Sfax.

2   Literature Review and Research Motivation

The management of road traffic congestion is used to optimize traffic management and improve transport infrastructure. The forecasting system is set up to know the status of the network in real time, reduce the risk of failure and quickly solve the possible problems of remote congestion. In the literature, several studies have shown the importance of road traffic management. The researchers proposed a SUA approach, which uses message exchanging to establish a communication protocol between vehicles. It searches for the shortest route based on historical observations, then computes travel time forecasts based on vehicle location in real-time [1]. To measure travel time in the congestion situation, the researchers used an approach to determine a robust itinerary in an urban transport network and to estimate the travel time on a road link, taking into account the dynamic aspects of traffic congestion [2]. In another logic, the researchers examined transport policies and practices on both the supply and demand sides and finds that indirect travel demand management might be the most desirable solution to this chronic traffic ailment. The concept of absorption of traffic demand through the renaissance of streets as a way for traffic relief is introduced from dense Asian urban contexts [3]. In Tunisia, the researchers proposed a Bayesian network (BN) analysis approach to modeling the probabilistic dependency structure of congestion causes on a particular road segment and analyzing the probability of traffic congestion in Sfax city. The BN method is used to analyze the uncertainty and probability of traffic congestion, and is proved to be fully capable of representing the stochastic nature of the road network situation [4].

According to a recent census of the Ministry of Equipment, Housing and Territorial Development of 2017, our work is based essentially on general traffic census data in the city of Sfax. The census data provide statistically reliable information on road traffic conditions and this encourages reflection for better exploitation of existing infrastructure and better management of traffic flows. With a view to improving traffic management, our contribution focuses on the adaptation of a method capable of both identifying the different relevant variables of road traffic, modeling the probabilistic dependence structure on a road segment, to analyze the probabilities of urban congestion, to measure the demand for travel and to simulate its contribution to urban congestion. The development of a road traffic management system is also used to model traffic movements inside in the city and to detect road axes that are often narrow and congested.

3 Road Traffic Design and Define Variables

Road traffic management systems should provide for traffic planning and regulation, this stage of the process is designed through macroscopic variables. Macroscopic models describe traffic at a high level of aggregation, the purpose of which is to repeatedly generate vehicle flows regardless of the component parts. These models are typically used for planning and control operations on large networks. The macroscopic models are based on the analogy with fluid dynamics and are more appropriate control laws to simulate a road flow over a large network. The traffic flow is supposed to be homogeneous and one-dimensional, the basic variables in the macroscopic model are traffic flow (Q), density (K) and average speed of the flow (ASF). The three variables (Q, K and V) are interconnected by traffic flow laws and are built on the same principle as the laws of fluid mechanics. The temporal evolution and spatial distribution of macroscopic quantities are managed by systems of nonlinear partial differential equations called conservation laws.

In the analysis of urban congestion, the traffic flow, the average speed and the density are therefore indispensable sources of data in the creation of a road traffic management system, and from these three indicators we can identify several other variables directly related to the theory of traffic flow. We draw a global portrait of road congestion in urban areas to compare the level of congestion of certain sections, with a view to targeting the most congested points in the road network. To achieve this objective, we identified four variables: Standard Time Delay (STD), Rate of travel speed (RTS), Road traffic situation (TS), and Traffic Volume (TV). The share of private cars (SPC) can be defined in the urban congestion analysis and track progress in traffic structure, a steady increase in motorized traffic leads to congestion traffic and a shortage of parking spaces in the city center [4]. The increase in the modal share of motorized trips has clearly increased the number of vehicle miles travelled, the flow decreases, the density increases and the average speed of the flow begins to decrease (the vehicles that join the traffic contribute to reduce the speed of circulation). The rate of travel speed is used to measure the difference between the flow speed and the free flow velocity (FFV), it also expresses the congestion level in the road network in relation to free flow conditions. In the case where the variable (TS) is close to 0, the rate of the movement speed is low, and the variable (RTS) is therefore in a fluid circulation situation. On the contrary, if the variable (RTS) is close to 1, then the traffic is probably in a saturated traffic situation and the roads are blocked. In order to estimate cumulative delays for a given section of road, it is necessary not only to know the speed profile of the vehicles moving on it, but also the number of vehicles likely to experience delays. In the opposite case of congestion, the traffic is in a so-called fluid state, there is little interaction between the vehicles, the safety distances are naturally respected, the speed is not influenced by the presence of other vehicles and the traffic volume is considerably lower than in the situation of congestion, as indicated in Table 1.

Table 1. Variables and state definitions for the proposed BN model [4]

Variable: Symbol	Description	Definition of states
Share of private cars (SPC)	The modal share of the car in percentage	Low: $\leq$ 80% High: > 81%
Traffic flow $Q(x,t)$	The number of vehicles (N) passing to the point (x) of a section between two instants (t_1) and (t_2), and describing the distribution of vehicles over time	Low: $\leq$ 1315 v/h High: > 1315 v/h
Density $K(x, t)$	The density $K(t, x_1, x_2)$ is defined by the number of vehicles (M) which are at the instant (t) in the section delimited by the points (x_1) and (x_2). Density describes the distribution of vehicles in space and is expressed in number of vehicles in kilometers	Low: $\leq$ 59 v/km High: > 59 v/km
Average speed of the flow (ASF)	It is the ratio between the flow rate and the density expressed by kilometer per hour (km/h).	Low: $\leq$ 15 km/h High: > 15 km/h
Free flow velocity (FFV)	The flow velocity is the free flow velocity without congestion	Low: $\leq$ 30 km/h High: > 30 km/h
Rate of travel speed (RTS)	This indicator expresses the level of congestion of a road section with respect to free flow conditions. It is a non-negative value and between 0 and 1: $RTS = \frac{V_{freeflowvelocity} - V_{theaveragespeedoftheflow}}{V_{freeflowvelocity}}$ (1)	Free: $\leq$ 0.5 Congestion: > 0.5
Standard time delay (STD)	It measures the hourly delay over a determined distance (hours per km) for each of the urban network segments from the following relationship. $STD = Q(x,t) \times \left(\frac{1}{ASF} - \frac{1}{FFV}\right)$ (2)	Low: $\leq$ 60 km/v High: > 60 km/v
Traffic volume (TV)	It gives an opinion on the intensity of circulation. The indicator is used to determine the volume in the road network.	Low: 0% High: 1%
Road traffic situation (RTS)	This indicator gives an idea of the quality of service of the roads	Class A: fluid Class B: dense Class C: congestion

4 Macroscopic Modeling

The flow of traffic can be modeled according to relations between the flow, the density and the average speed of the flow. The Greenshields model, presented in [5] and [6], allows presenting a macroscopic model in two separate figures. Figure (1) illustrates the function $ASF = f(Q)$ and Fig. (2) illustrates the relationship $ASF = f(K)$. According to the Greenshields diagram, the flow level corresponds two distinct possible values (q_0, q_1), when the flow rate is low ($q_0 = qmax \times 0.75 = 1164$ veh/h), the speed can reach its maximum and also can reach at its minimum. The intersection between (q_0) and the traffic flow gives a new velocity point (V_1) which corresponds to the minimum speed under extreme congestion conditions. The intersection between q_1 ($q_1 = qmax \times 0.9 = 1400$ veh/h) and the flow gives the maximum permissible speed for road transport. The flow rate is therefore a quadratic function of the flow speed, which gives a parabolic shape with a point of inflection around V_O (21 km/h). When the concentration is low between [0, K_1 = 37 veh/km], the number of vehicles on a section is very limited, the vehicles do not interact and each one can circulate at the desired speed called the free flow speed (Vf = 42 km/h), and in this case the circulation is fluid. When the density increases between [K_1, K_2 = 111 veh/km], the interactions become more important and the speeds practiced decrease between [V_1 = 11, V_2 = 30] km/h and in this case the traffic will be dense. In the extreme case where the section is highly congested, the concentration has gone up by more than 147 veh/km, and the average speed of circulation is less than or equal to 11 km/h.

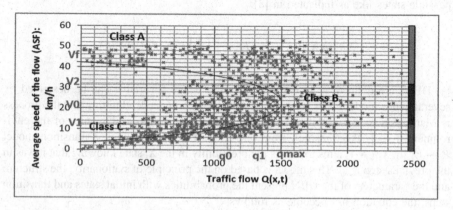

Fig. 1. Relation between traffic flow and ASF. The relation allows to identify the different situation of the road traffic system.

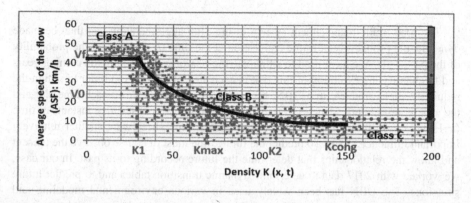

Fig. 2. Relation between density and ASF. The relation allows to identify the different situation of the road traffic system.

5 Dynamic Bayes Model

5.1 Congestion Management Solutions

The construction of a dynamic Bayesian model represent the evolution of variables over time. Various approaches have been suggested to present à DBN, Markov hidden models and Kálmán filter models are the most used models in dynamic reasoning. A dynamic or temporal BN, often denoted as DBN, makes it possible to represent the evolution of the random variables of road traffic with time steps [7].

Generally, an DBN encodes the joint probability distribution of variables $X[t] = X_1[t], ..., X_N[t]$, and can be considered as a static BN roll with T × N variables. Due to the nature of the systems, we can define the joined probability distribution on the set of possible states like as indicated in [8]:

$$X[t] = X_1[t], ..., Xn[T] = \prod_{i=1}^{T} \prod_{i=1}^{n} p(X_i[t]/Pa(X_i[t])) \tag{3}$$

DBNs are defined as an extension of BN, where a variable can be described by several nodes modeling its behavior at several times. Indeed, admitting that the process is Markovian model and it is invariant in time. The temporal dynamics of the environment models the transition from one slice of time to another, a transition model $P \rightarrow (X_i[t]/X_i[t-1]$ aims to model the probability in the X_t state knowing that it was in the previous step X_{t-1}. This model is based on the principle of stationarity, the structure and the parameters of the DBN present the probabilities with initial states and transition steps, the equation has become as follows:

$$P(X_1[t], ..., Xn[T]) = P_1(X_1[t]) \prod_{t=2}^{T-1} P \rightarrow (X_i[t]/X_i[t-1]) \tag{4}$$

The road traffic management system in the Sfax agglomeration can then be made dynamic, the probability of traffic congestion at the time (t) depends on the probability of the past ($t-1$). We have tried to anticipate the risk of congestion in the coming years and to quantify the evolution of this risk in each step of the time, in order to obtain the required target variables. In a DBN, the variables are connected to each time slot and the arcs represent dependencies of transitions between two consecutive instants of time ($t-1$) and (t). In the construction of DBN models, time slices were another relatively important influence factor. To predict the future, one must of course observe the present and know the relationships that determine the future according to its past. In our case, we worked with 2017 data to determine dynamic transition tables and to predict future situations. The DBN has been widely used in various environmental modeling and decision support applications, which provides a method for modeling complex systems

[9]. According to the general circulation census, data aggregations were carried out at a five-year rate to assess road traffic indicators and to assess the economic function of road links, the time is set by a step of 5 years. We chose to predict 2 time slices corresponding to the years 2022 and 2027 respectively, and the results of the simu-.lation are shown in Fig. 3.

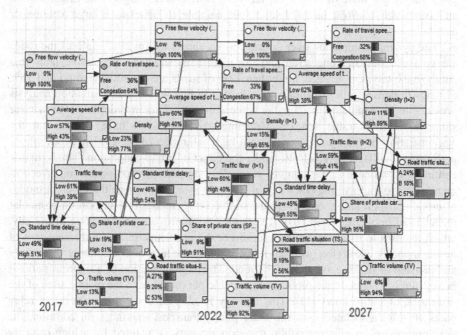

Fig. 3. Dynamic simulation of a Bayesian network. The dynamic simulation results indicate that there is heavy congestion over a 10-year horizon.

6 Result of the Dynamic Simulation

The dynamic simulation contains the simulation of the dynamic flow and movement conditions. The principle is to be able to predict the traffic situation and especially to obtain simulated traffic data of various natures, such as the flow rate, the average flow speed, the density, etc. Dynamic simulation is classically interested in sections of the network that can quantify traffic congestion by measuring the overall functioning of the network. This step allows for the analysis and evaluation of road traffic variables over time and allows the analysis of possible inputs of dynamic traffic management system. In the majority of cases, a DBN is used to analyze scenarios of major road events (estimating the modal share of private transport, the delay due to traffic congestion, etc.). This makes it possible to set up traffic management plans, using a catalog of scenarios to improve the structure of the road network and the strategy and to limit the disadvantages. This allows a better understanding of the road network while facilitating decision-making. In this context, the DBN model allows to conduct an analysis of different scenarios of urban mobility evolution. The results showed that the traffic situation is getting worse each year, the probability of a congestion situation is 69% in 2027, the modal share of private car has been increased at a higher rate of congestion and can reach to 96% in 2027, that will be able to generate a large volume of circulation.

The dynamic simulation over 2 time periods shows that in 2017, 53% of the roads are in a situation of congestion and the main axes showed some traffic jams that paralyze the city. On average, more than 13% of roads are classified as fluid and 18% of roads in dense traffic situations, as indicated in Fig. 4. The traffic situation analysis provides traffic regulators with traffic forecasting functions in order to obtain a clear situation of road traffic service. Modeling and simulation have shown that the agglomeration of Sfax has experienced a high saturation of the road network whose performance collapse dramatically under the effect of urban congestion. This situation continues to worsen in the coming years. We subsequently proposed some recommendations to improve the efficiency of transport systems between the different modes of urban transport and to encourage the use of anther modes of transport, in particular the share of public transport [10]. It is capable to improve the functioning of the city, which requires to try and provide solutions to the problems. First, the management of traffic is poorly controlled (as today), for example the lack of control over the supply and demand of parking, on and off the road. The implementation of a rigorous parking policy aim is to remedy the problem of anarchic parking, one of the main causes of the disruption of traffic flows [11]. This strategy is adopted by setting up a set of relay parks (P + R) associated with the main public transport interfaces. In addition, the development of an efficient public transport network, structured by a high-capacity primary network of geometrical structure is a necessary element to reduce the congestion of city streets. The reorganization of the transport of goods in town is also inevitable, especially to control the parking of trucks (including long-term parking). The idea is directly related to developing new logistics platforms using a retail goods, delivery policy adapted to its needs. Finally, the reduction of car traffic (the most energy-consuming mode, and the most pollution) is generated by the regulation, the direction of the traffic and also by the increase of the share of the less polluting modes of transport, and the least noisy, this goal cannot be achieved with-out providing alternative solutions to the private car, namely: specific site public transport projects (tramways), the proliferation of pedestrian streets and the establishment of a public system to encourage the use of the bike share service.

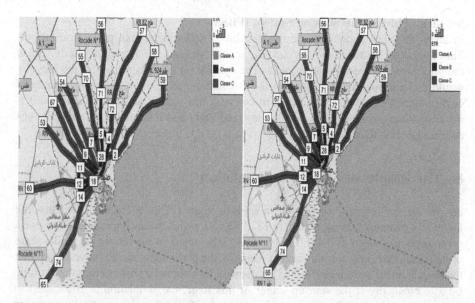

Fig. 4. The prediction results of the traffic situation in 2022 and 2027 (respectively). The red path shows the situation of congestion (class C), the blue path illustrates the dense traffic situations (class B), and the green way illustrates the fluidity situation (Class A). (Color figure online)

7 The Creation of Scenarios

We have developed an application to predict road congestion situation over a five- to ten-year horizon. The main challenge for the road network is to study scenarios in which it will be necessary to improve the management of road traffic and to reduce congestion on the streets in the Sfax city. The generated scenarios are therefore distinguished at the level of the structuring supply and the envisaged demand. In succession, two solutions have been predetermined by the public authorities to illustrate situations, to significantly reduce congestion and increase traffic speed.

Scenario A: specific site public transport projects (SSPTP):
In 2013, the Ministry of Transport developed a feasibility study for an environmentally sustainable transport system in the agglomeration of Sfax. This study recommended a public transport network characterized as follows:

- 2 tram lines (T1 and T2). The first line T1 is a line of trams on a west/north axis, with a frequency of 5 min during peak periods. The second line T2 is a tram line on a city center/north axis. The first phase in 2020 will include a section of the 13.5 km of tram line.
- 3 BHNS lines: a structuring service provided by high-level service buses (HLSB, modern vehicles with capacity for 160 people) operating on a dedicated site, with a high level of priority. This service is broken down into 3 lines. BH3 is a line of BHNS3 on a Southwest/East axis, with a frequency of 5 min. BH4 is a line of BHNS on a city center/northwest axis with a frequency of 7 min. BH5 is a BHNS line with a city center/north-east axis, with a frequency of 4 min [12].

Scenario: Public Bike Sharing System (PBSS)
In 2019, the Sfax regional authority launched a self-service bike promotion project. This project is broken down by several actions such as the feasibility study, urban mobility plan and bicycle path project. The orientation towards the use of the bicycles would make it possible to decongest the circulation and to avoid a certain number of environmental nuisances. Generally, this system has created several advantages, it is not expensive, available permanently, day, and night and is available by subscriptions as for all public transport.

8   The Results of Scenarios Simulation

As part of the scenario simulation, the PDU report (PDU 2016) estimated that the number of passengers is equivalent to 137,053,550, which makes it possible to achieve a revenue per passenger of 0.471 TND by 2030. This scenario can reduce the modal share of light traffic by 30%. For the second scenario, the preliminary studies have shown that the bicycle rental system can reduce the demand for the modal share of motorized traffic by 5%, especially at the start-up stage. At this stage, the simulation is established to evaluate the impact of the two scenarios on road traffic and more specifically on traffic congestion and it is therefore necessary to know exactly the probability of having congestion knowing that the scenario (A) or/and the scenario (B) are carried out one after the other or simultaneously. According to [12], scenario (B) will be achieved at the beginning of 2020 with a reduction of the light traffic share by 5%. Scenario (A) will be carried out at the beginning of the year 2021 with a reduction estimate of the light traffic share of 30%. However, we have adjusted on the variable (SPC) for each time step and with the predefined scenarios, as indicated in Table 2.

Table 2. The predefined scenarios of the SPC variable

Variable	2017	2022	2022	2027	2027
Share of private cars (SPC)	Simulation results	Simulation results without scenarios	Simulation results with scenario B	Simulation results without scenarios	Simulation results with scenarios A + B
Low (%)	17	8	22	4	57
High (%)	83	92	78	96	43

Simulation models provide information on traffic congestion, which we can know their probability distribution. At each iteration or at each moment of time, the DBN simulated the model and the probability distributions are evolved along with the predefined scenarios. In this case, urban transport systems are characterized by a growing congestion situation of urban roads caused by the massive increase in car traffic. This situation is progressively evolving towards a heavily congested network. It seems to think about palliative solutions intended, and to improve the organization of the displacements. For this raison, new political orientations are to be envisaged, the policy of promotion of the bicycle and the realization of a tramway put in place involving combined influences on the daily movements. In the simulation results after integrating two possible scenarios, we observed dramatic changes in the outcome variables. The PBSS scenario simulation achieves an improvement in the average speed of 7% in 2022, and it also reduces the congestion situation by 8%. On the contrary, the simulation of the two scenarios (PBSS + SSPTP) demonstrated a very high level of performance and scalability, with a measured efficiency of 22% at the variable level of average speed of the flow (*ASF*) and 23% of the level on the road traffic situation (*RTS*). This reduction in light traffic is due to the increase in the modal share of public transport, which implies that these scenarios make it possible to relieve the critical situation of road traffic in the Sfax urban area, and in this case, the city becomes more compact in its spatial, social and environmental dimension.

9 Discussion and Conclusion

The problems of road transport are therefore numerous and have been the subject of much analysis. Precisely because of the current congestion situation, we should focus on specific recommendations and initiatives to reduce road congestion and its impacts. To decongest the city's streets, it is necessary to reduce the motorized traffic share by 54%, and the public authorities have made to change the current traffic policy and to establish an adequate traffic policy favoring sustainable transport, PBSS, or developing restraint automobile demand, such as the creation of green zones (limited by 30 km/h), urban charging, congestion charges, parking policies and the removal of lanes. In addition, the creation and deployment of a new generation of the transport system are essential. Technology-based approaches include a variety of measures that can improve traffic flow, improve road safety and reduce congestion [13]. The research objectives are to streamline the flow of traffic during peak demand periods and when the road temporarily loses some of its capacity. The congestion analysis was followed by a systemic analysis of the congestion regulations, it was to check when the congestion became more intense and how it can be remedied. We therefore wanted to know the higher degree of congestion that was related to both a predetermined reduction in the modal share of public transit (the lack of performance) and a remarkable increase in the use of the private car. More generally, given the increase in traffic congestion and the problems of mobility of road traffic, we proposed to abandon the car as often as possible and to use public transport or so-called soft modes bikes, walking) [14]. The future shows us if the alternatives are sufficiently attractive and if the citizens follow these proposals for improvement. The limit of our work depends on the reliability and lack of statistical data as a starting point for developing further study in the analysis of traffic congestion. In the first part, we encountered problems related in particular to the lack of identification indicators that aim to directly measure the magnitudes of congestion. The methodological framework proposed can be broadened to incorporate the effect of other cognitive factors involved in road traffic (estimation of travel time, deletion of offenses, risk factors and accident prevention). The unavailability of instantaneous data played a leading role in the establishment of the complete Bayesian model covering all types of current and real-time problems.

The future work looks at different perspectives, a mobile application can be programmed to avoid congestion related traffic in the city of Sfax. This application helps drivers to manage their movements and helps to avoid traffic jams, while offering traffic and driving assistance solutions. We can also develop a predictive analysis in order to prevent in real time traffic jams and accidents related to urban congestion.

References

1. Jamal, R.: Road traffic congestion management based on a search-allocation approach. J. Transp. Telecommun. Inst. **18**(2), 25–33 (2017). https://doi.org/10.1515/ttj-2017-0003
2. Lamia, K., Abdellah, D., Azedine, B.: Robust routing based on urban traffic congestion patterns. Procedia Comput. Sci. **109**, 698–703 (2017). https://doi.org/10.1016/j.procs.2017.05.380
3. Wen L., Kenworthy, J., Guo, X., Marinova, D.: Solving traffic congestion through street renaissance: a perspective from Dense Asian cities. Urban Sci. Special Issue Sustainable Place Making and Urban Governance (2018). https://doi.org/10.3390/urbansci3010018
4. Derbel, A., Boujelbene, Y.: Road congestion analysis in the agglomeration of Sfax using a Bayesian model. In: Boudriga, N., Alouini, M.-S., Rekhis, S., Sabir, E., Pollin, S. (eds.) UNet 2018. LNCS, vol. 11277, pp. 131–142. Springer, Cham (2018). https://doi.org/10.1007/978-3-030-02849-7_12
5. Wen-Long, J.: Nonstandard second-order formulation of the LWR model. Transportmetrca B: Transp. Dyn. **7**(1) 2019. https://doi.org/10.1080/21680566.2019.1617803
6. Abedelkareem, A., Mario, M., Stefania, S.: A dynamic mesoscopic network loading model for spillback queuing assessment. In: IEEE International Conference on Environment and Electrical Engineering and IEEE Industrial and Commercial Power Systems Europe (EEEIC/I&CPS Europe) (2019). https://doi.org/10.1109/eeeic.2019.8783258
7. Derbel, A., Boujelbene, Y.: Bayesian network for traffic management application: estimated the travel time. In: 2015 2nd World Symposium on Web Applications and Networking (WSWAN), Sousse, pp. 1–6 (2015). https://doi.org/10.1109/wswan.2015.7210328
8. Wen, Y., et al.: Semantic modelling of ship behavior in harbor based on ontology and dynamic bayesian network. ISPRS Int. J. Geo-Inf. **8**(3), 107 (2019). https://doi.org/10.3390/ijgi8030107
9. Fan, X., Zhang, J., Shen, Q.: Prediction of road congestion diffusion based on dynamic bayesian networks. J/ Phys.: Conf. Ser. **1176** (2019). https://doi.org/10.1088/1742-6596/1176/2/022046. Computer Science
10. Boujelbene, Y., Derbel, A.: The performance analysis of public transport operators in Tunisia Using AHP method. Procedia Comput. Sci. **73**, 498–508 (2015)
11. Boujelbene, Y., Derbel, A.: The performance analysis of public transport operators in Tunisia using ER approach. Global J. Manag. Bus. Res. **16**(1) (2016)
12. Charfi, F., Stratégie Sfax 2030: Diagnostic stratégique de l'état du développement de la région, ADSS, 2016. http://festunis.org/media/2015/pdf/Publication_Strategie_Sfax2030.pdf
13. Derbel, A., Boujelbene, Y.: Development an approach to fusion of an anti-collision system. In: International Conference on Advanced Logistics and Transport (ICALT) (2014). https://doi.org/10.1109/icadlt.2014.6864080
14. Derbel, A., Boujelbene, Y.: Automatic classification and analysis of multiple-criteria decision making. In: Bouhlel, M.S., Rovetta, S. (eds.) SETIT 2018. SIST, vol. 146, pp. 83–93. Springer, Cham (2020). https://doi.org/10.1007/978-3-030-21005-2_8

Energy Efficient Target Coverage in Wireless Sensor Networks Using Adaptive Learning

Ashish Rauniyar[1,2], Jeevan Kunwar[1], Hårek Haugerud[1], Anis Yazidi[1(✉)], and Paal Engelstad[1,2]

[1] Autonomous System and Network Research Group,
Department of Computer Science, Oslo Metropolitan University, Oslo, Norway
anisy@oslomet.no
[2] Department of Technology Systems, University of Oslo, Oslo, Norway

Abstract. Over the past few years, innovation in the development of Wireless Sensor Networks (WSNs) has evolved rapidly. WSNs are being used in many application fields such as target coverage, battlefield surveillance, home security, health care supervision, and many more. However, power usage in WSNs remains a challenging issue due to the low capacity of batteries and the difficulty of replacing or charging them, especially in harsh environments. Therefore, this has led to the development of various architectures and algorithms to deal with optimizing the energy usage of WSNs. In particular, extending the lifetime of the WSN in the context of target coverage problems by resorting to intelligent scheduling has received a lot of research attention. In this paper, we propose a scheduling technique for WSN based on a novel concept within the theory of Learning Automata (LA) called pursuit LA. Each sensor node in the WSN is equipped with an LA so that it can autonomously select its proper state, i.e., either sleep or active with the aim to cover all targets with the lowest energy cost. Through comprehensive experimental testing, we verify the efficiency of our algorithm and its ability to yield a near-optimal solution. The results are promising, given the low computational footprint of the algorithm.

Keywords: Wireless Sensor Network · Adaptive learning · Learning Automata · Minimum active sensors · Target coverage · Energy efficiency

1 Introduction

Wireless Sensor Networks (WSNs) consist of a large number of identical and independent sensors being deployed either in a random manner or in a deterministic manner for effective monitoring of an area of the region of interest. The sensor nodes are the principal components of the WSNs. Usually, these sensor nodes are small, low power devices that have the ability to communicate

© Springer Nature Switzerland AG 2020
I. Jemili and M. Mosbah (Eds.): DiCES-N 2019, CCIS 1130, pp. 133–147, 2020.
https://doi.org/10.1007/978-3-030-40131-3_9

over a short distance. The three major operations of these sensors are sensing, processing, and communication. WSNs admit a large list of applications that cover almost any field [20]. WSN technology has it first roots in the military domain, where it was used for developing applications for effective monitoring, surveillance of the battlefield, etc. WSNs also admit other domain applications involving home monitoring, health care, temperature, disaster prevention, environmental monitoring, pollution, and so on.

An effective power management factor is one of the keys elements for enhancing the lifetime of a WSN. Batteries that are used in a sensor network are relatively small in size and therefore possess a low power storage capacity. These batteries need either a replacement or frequent recharging for continuous network operation. However, this is impractical in many real-life situations as those sensors might be deployed in areas that are difficult to access. The network lifetime is defined in the context of network coverage problems as the duration of time elapsed from the network starts functioning with full coverage from its initialization to the time instant where the coveted coverage criteria is unsatisfied [12].

There have been many research works addressing the problem of inefficient energy consumption in WSNs. More particularly, a significant amount of research has been conducted for energy-efficient data aggregation and dissemination, transmission power control and nodes activity scheduling, energy-aware routing for efficient utilization of the energy in WSNs [4].

Another important aspect of the WSNs used for monitoring purposes is the coverage area of the WSN. This area can be defined as the area within which a sensor node is able to monitor and track the specified target's activities. Intuitively, each target should be monitored by at least one of the sensor node continuously, such that there is continuity in the network operation. Generally, the network lifetime can be enhanced by scheduling the activity of each of the sensor nodes in either active state or sleep state [4]. For energy-efficient scheduling, each sensor in the network has two modes, *active* mode, and *sleep* mode. The nodes are scheduled intelligently so that they can alternate between those two modes while meeting the desired coverage requirement.

The target coverage problem by the sensor nodes in the WSN includes three families of problems which are defined as follows according to [13]:

- **Area Coverage**
  This coverage problem is concerned with the monitoring of the targets in the entire area of the network.
- **Target Coverage**
  This coverage problem is concerned with the monitoring of only certain targets within the specified region of the network.
- **Barrier Coverage**
  The barrier coverage problem aims rather to minimize the probability of undetected penetration through the barrier in the network.

There is a vast amount of research on coverage problems for designing energy-efficient WSN. Many scheduling algorithms have been proposed to schedule the activity of the sensor nodes. One of the scheduling methods for energy-efficient WSN is through Learning Automata (LA) [13,16]. This mechanism provides the sensor node to learn their state and select its appropriate state, i.e. either active or sleep mode, for the purpose of prolonging the network lifetime of the WSNs.

In order to prolong the network lifetime, this paper mainly deals with the problem of area coverage using the theory of LA. Although the theory of LA has been applied before to solve the problem of area coverage, our solution enjoys some desirable designed properties compared to [13]. In fact, we apply LA to each of the sensors to determine each state: active or sleep. Therefore, we opt to pursue the joint action of the team LA corresponding to the best solution found so far using the concept of pursuit learning [1,17,22]. Our proposed scheme is different from the work of [13] as the LA update of latter work does not track the best solution found so far. In [13], the authors implemented a reward and penalty mechanism in the following manner:

- Reward action sleep - if all targets of the sensor are covered. In other word, taking the opposite action, which is active, would not result in any benefit.
- Reward action activate - if the sensor in question covers at least one target exclusively. In other words, taking the opposite action, which is sleep, will result in at least one less target that can not be covered.

The remainder of this paper is organized as follows. In Sect. 2, we survey the related work and introduce some background concepts about the theory of LA, which is an essential component in our solution. Section 3 details the main approach for solving the sensor coverage problem, which is based on the theory of LA. In Sect. 4, we report some representative simulations results showing the efficiency of our scheme. Finally, we give some final conclusions in Sect. 5.

2   Background and Related Work

In this section, we shall review some basic concepts about the theory of Learning Automata (LA), which is fundamental for the understanding of our paper. Furthermore, we shall survey some pertinent related works.

2.1   Learning Automata

In the field of Automata Theory, an automaton [10,14,15,18,19] is characterized as a quintuple made out of a set of states, a set of outputs or actions, an input, a function that maps the present state and the input to the following state, and a function that maps a present state (and input) into the current output.

Definition 1: A LA is defined by a quintuple $\langle A, B, Q, F(.,.), G(.) \rangle$, where:

1. $A = \{\alpha_1, \alpha_2, \ldots, \alpha_r\}$ is the set of outputs or actions that the LA must choose from. $\alpha(t)$ is the action picked by the automaton at any moment or instant t.

2. $B = \{\beta_1, \beta_2, \ldots, \beta_m\}$ is the set of inputs or feedback to the automaton. $\beta(t)$ is the feedback at any moment t corresponding to the chosen action. The set B can be limited or unbounded. The most widely recognized LA input information is $B = \{0, 1\}$, where $\beta = 0$ represents reward or equivalently a positive feedback, and $\beta = 1$ represents penalty or equivalently a negative feedback.

3. $Q = \{q_1, q_2, \ldots, q_s\}$ is the set of finite states, where $Q(t)$ signifies the condition of the automaton at any moment t.

4. $F(.,.) : Q \times B \mapsto Q$ is a mapping as far as the state and input at the moment t, with the end goal that, $q(t+1) = F[q(t), \beta(t)]$. It is known as a *transition function*, i.e., a function that decides the condition of the automaton at any resulting time instant $t+1$. This mapping can either be deterministic or stochastic.

5. $G(.)$: is a mapping $G : Q \mapsto A$, and is known as the *output function*. G decides the action taken by the automaton in the event that it is in a given state as: $\alpha(t) = G[q(t)]$.

If the sets Q, B and A are all finite, the automaton is said to be *finite*.

The Environment, E, ordinarily, alludes to the medium where the automaton functions. The Environment has all the outer variables that influence the activities of the automaton. Mathematically, an Environment can be preoccupied with a triple $\langle A, C, B \rangle$. A, C, and B are characterized as follows:

1. $A = \{\alpha_1, \alpha_2, \ldots, \alpha_r\}$ is the set of actions.

2. $B = \{\beta_1, \beta_2, \ldots, \beta_m\}$ is the output set of the Environment. Once more, we consider the situation when $m = 2$, i.e., with $\beta = 0$ representing a "Reward", and $\beta = 1$ representing a "Penalty".

3. $C = \{c_1, c_2, \ldots, c_r\}$ is a set of punishment or penalty probabilities, where component $c_i \in C$ relates to an input activity α_i.

The way toward learning depends on a learning loop, including the two entities: the Random Environment (RE), and the LA, as depicted in Fig. 1. In the learning procedure, the LA persistently communicates with the Environment to process reactions to its different activities (i.e., its decisions). Finally, through adequate communications, the LA endeavors to gain proficiency with the ideal action offered by the RE. The real procedure of learning is represented as a set of associations or interactions between the RE and the LA.

The automaton is offered a set of actions, and it is obliged to picking one of them. At the point when an action is chosen among the pool of actions, the Environment gives out a response $\beta(t)$ at a time "t". The automaton is either penalized or rewarded with an obscure likelihood c_i or $1 - c_i$, separately. Based on the response $\beta(t)$, the state of the automaton $\phi(t)$ is updated and another new action is picked at (t+1). The penalty probability c_i satisfies:

$$c_i = \Pr[\beta(t) = 1 | \alpha(t) = \alpha_i] \qquad (i = 1, 2, \ldots, r). \tag{1}$$

We now present a few of the significant definitions utilized in the field. $P(t)$ is alluded to as the action probability vector, where, $P(t) =$

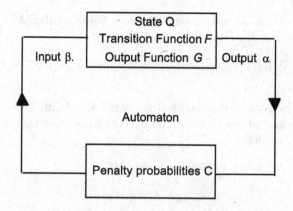

Fig. 1. Feedback loop of LA.

$[p_1(t), p_2(t), \ldots, p_r(t)]^T$, in which every component of the vector:

$$p_i(t) = \Pr[\alpha(t) = \alpha_i], \ i = 1, \ldots, r, \ \text{such that} \ \sum_{i=1}^{r} p_i(t) = 1 \ \forall t. \tag{2}$$

Given an action probability vector, $P(t)$ at time t, the *average penalty* is:

$$
\begin{aligned}
M(t) &= E[\beta(t)|P(t)] = \Pr[\beta(t) = 1|P(t)] \\
&= \sum_{i=1}^{r} \Pr[\beta(t) = 1|\alpha(t) = \alpha_i] \ Pr[\alpha(t) = \alpha_i] \\
&= \sum_{i=1}^{r} c_i p_i(t).
\end{aligned}
\tag{3}
$$

The average penalty for the "pure-chance" automaton is given by:

$$M_0 = \frac{1}{r} \sum_{i=1}^{r} c_i. \tag{4}$$

As $t \mapsto \infty$, if the average penalty $M(t) < M_0$, in any event asymptotically, the automaton is commonly viewed as superior to the pure-chance automaton. $E[M(t)]$ is given by:

$$E[M(t)] = E\{E[\beta(t)|P(t)]\} = E[\beta(t)]. \tag{5}$$

A LA that performs better than by pure-chance is said to be *expedient*.

Definition 2: A LA is considered *expedient* if:

$$\lim_{t \to \infty} E[M(t)] < M_0.$$

Definition 3: A LA is said to be *absolutely expedient* if $E[M(t+1)|P(t)] < M(t)$, implying that $E[M(t+1)] < E[M(t)]$.

Definition 4: A LA is considered *optimal* if $\lim_{t \to \infty} E[M(t)] = c_l$, where $c_l = \min_i \{c_i\}$.

It ought to be noticed that no ideal LA exist. Marginally sub-optimal performance, also termed above as ϵ-optimal execution, is what that LA researchers endeavor to accomplish.

Definition 5: A LA is considered ϵ-*optimal* if:

$$\lim_{n \to \infty} E[M(t)] < c_l + \epsilon, \tag{6}$$

where $\epsilon > 0$, and can be arbitrarily small, by a reasonable choice of some parameter of the LA.

2.2   Related Works

The authors in [6] use a probabilistic coverage model that takes the distance parameter for the target coverage. This algorithm is based on the modified weighted set, which helps to organize sensors into disjoint and non-disjoint set covers. In the study reported in [23], the authors introduce the concept of coverage-centric nodes. Coverage-centric nodes are the nodes that ensure larger coverage than the other nodes. In this regard, a novel algorithm called the Coverage-Centric Active Nodes Selection (CCANS) algorithm was devised. This algorithm depends on the formation of the Connected Dominating Set (CDS). The active nodes of the network structure the CDS. This provides the backbone to other nodes for sensing and communication purposes such that the data communication is processed through this route.

The work in [21] investigated the application of the sleep and awake schedule to the low duty cycle WSNs. In particular, the author of the latter study has taken into consideration of the explicit effect of synchronization error for designing the sleep and awake schedule. The proposed scheme in this work is divided into two main parts. The first part of the work provides a sleep and awake schedule by the use of an efficient search method for optimizing the number of sensors to ensure target coverage. In the second part, the authors focus on optimizing the quality of service of the network.

The work in [9] provides a heuristic and artificial bee colony algorithm as a scheduling technique. Through their experiments, the authors concluded that their methods help in improving the network lifetime of the sensor networks.

There is a vast majority of the literature that can be found about the target coverage problem of the WSNs. In [11], the authors have discussed the target coverage along with the data collection problem in WSNs. The authors investigate the use of polynomial-time approximation and polynomial-time constant approximation methods to analyze the complexity of different approaches for target coverage problems.

In [3], the sensor nodes are organized into several maximal set covers. These set covers are activated to monitor the targets, while the other set of nodes remains in sleep mode to save the energy. The main goal of [3] was to find the disjoint set of sensor nodes for energy conservation to increase the network lifetime. The authors have used the heuristic approach for computing the sets through the use of linear programming. The result shows that there is an increase in the lifetime with an increase in the target and sensing range with a specified number of targets. A heuristic method for organizing sensor nodes into disjoint set covers is carried out in [2,8]. The sensor set that is in the active state can only monitor the targets, and the other sensor set goes into low energy sleep mode. Also, the authors in [8] have used greedy Connected Set Coverage (CSC) heuristics algorithm to increase the network operation lifetime.

In the case of the mobile target, it is difficult to find the exact coverage and the position of the targets in a large-scale WSNs. In a practical scenario, sensor sensing follows a probabilistic sensing mode. In [5], the authors have proposed a probabilistic sensing model and circular graph for detecting the mobile targets. They have formulated a probabilistic trap coverage with maximum network lifetime problem. The authors also discussed circular coverage graph problem for determining whether a given sensor network can provide the probabilistic trap coverage or not.

3   Proposed Adaptive Learning Algorithm

3.1   Problem Formulation

Let us consider that there are a set of M targets denoted by $T = \{T_1, T_2, ...T_M\}$ which are being monitored by set of N sensor nodes S denoted by $S = \{S_1, S_2, ...S_N\}$. These two sets are deployed in a $X \times X$ area. All sensor nodes have a fixed sensing range "R". Also, we assume that there is the number of sensor nodes exceeds the number of targets. In order to increase the lifetime of the network, a scheduling algorithm has been proposed in this paper. A target point T_j within the range $1 \leq j \leq M$, is said to be covered by a sensor node if it falls inside this range of one of the sensor nodes $1 \leq i \leq N$ [13].

Figure 2 shows the Venn diagram of the sensors and the targets with their bipartite graph. There are four sensors S1, S2, S3, and S4 with their respective targets T1, T2, T3, and T4. The circle with different colors represents the coverage of each of the sensor nodes. The bipartite graph shows the relationship between the sensors and the number of covered targets by them. We can observe that by only activating two sensors: S2 and S3, we can cover all the targets. The complexity of the problem increases exponentially as we increase the number of sensors since the number of possible configurations of N sensors in active and sleep modes is 2^N.

3.2   Adaptive Learning Algorithm

We have used the LA algorithm for scheduling the sensor nodes. We shall now delineate the details of our algorithm, which helps in finding the best active set

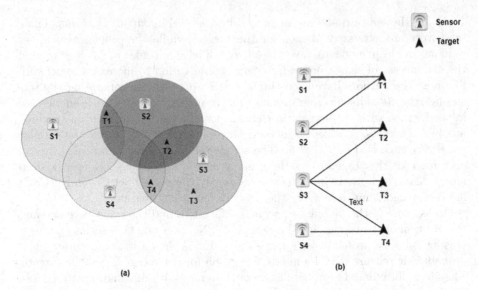

Fig. 2. (a) Sensors coverage with their targets and (b) Bipartite graph of sensors and targets (Color figure online)

of sensors that are monitoring the maximum number of targets at any given instant. As in [13], the actual flow of the algorithm is divided into three phases, which include an initial stage, a learning phase, and the target monitoring phase. We shall now focus on the initial phase and the learning phase. The monitoring phase is identical to the one presented in [13], and therefore, it is omitted here for the sake of brevity.

Initial Phase: In this phase, each sensor node in the network are provided with LA, which helps the sensor node to select its state either to active or sleep. In the initial stage, both states are equally probable, i.e., the probability of selecting either of the active or sleep state is initialized to be 0.5. Here, sensor nodes are endowed with a certain level of autonomy permitting to establish communication, transfer messages, including their ID, position, and list of covered targets with their neighbor node autonomously. This phase is followed by the learning phase and the target monitoring phase.

Learning Phase: In the learning phase, each of the sensor nodes is equipped with LA. At first, the node is selected randomly. Using LA, each node selects its state. Then it broadcasts the message packet, including its all information to the rest of the sensor nodes.

We attach to each of the N sensors a LA. For instance, let us consider the senor S_i. The automaton's state probability vector at the node i at time t is $P_i(t) = [p_{(i,1)}(t), p_{(i,2)}(t)]$.

Algorithm 1. Learning Phase

Best coverage set $= \emptyset$
For each LA action set initial probability $= 0.5$
for Every sensor node in the network **do**
    Choose random action for sensor node
end for
for iteration $= 0$ to max iterations **do**
    for Every sensor node in the network **do**
        Node $=$ choose an action according to LA
        Update Current LA actions
        if Node state $=$ Active **then**
            Current coverage set $=$ Current coverage $\bigcup$ node
        end if
    end for
    if |Current coverage set| $>$ |Best Coverage set| **then**
        Best coverage set $=$ Current coverage set
        Best LA actions $=$ Current LA actions
    end if
    for Every node in the network **do**
        if Best LA action of node is sleep **then**
            Decrease the probability to be active
        else
            Increase the probability of the node to be active
        end if
    end for
end for

Thus, $p_{(i,j)}(t)$ is the probability at time instant t to select an action j. In our settings, we have two actions: sleep or active. For the sake of notation, let us denote 0 as the action sleep, and 1 denote the action active.

The feedback function is a binary function which yields a reward whenever the coverage has been improved. This is denoted by |Current coverage set| $>$ |Best coverage set| in Algorithm 1. In more simple terms, if the aggregate state of the sensors chosen by the team of N LA yields an improvement in the coverage, which means covering more number of targets, the joint action of the LA that yielded that solution is rewarded by increasing the probability of the actions which formed that particular solution.

Let $J = \{j_1(t), j_2(t), ..., j_N(t)\}$ denote the action taken by the team of LA. Let $J^* = \{j_1^*(t), j_2^*(t), ..., j_N^*(t)\}$ be the best aggregate action of the team of LA so far yielding the highest coverage.

Thus, the idea of pursuit here is to reward the LA whose aggregate action is the highest possible so far, i.e., till the time instant t.

We consider the LA update equations at node i. The update is given by:

$$p_{(i,j)}(t+1) = (1-\lambda)\delta_{(i,j)} + \lambda p_{(i,j)}(t) \tag{7}$$

$$\delta_{(i,j)} = \begin{cases} 1 & \text{if } j = j_i^*(t) \\ 0 & \text{else} \end{cases} \tag{8}$$

λ is the update parameter and is time-independent.

The informed reader would observe that the above update scheme corresponds to the Linear-Reward Inaction LA update [16]. The pursuit paradigm we apply in this paper is an adaptation of the PolyLA-Pursuit scheme [7] recently proposed by Goodwin and Yazidi in the context of Machine Learning classification problems.

If $j \neq j_i^*(t)$ then $p_{(i,j)}(t+1)$ is reduced by multiplying by λ, which is less than 1.

$$p_{(i,j)}(t+1) = \lambda p_{(i,j)}(t) \tag{9}$$

However, if $j = j_i^*(t)$, then $p_{(i,j)}(t+1)$ is increased by:

$$p_{(i,j)}(t+1) - p_{(i,j)}(t) = [(1-\lambda) + \lambda p_{(i,j)}(t)] - p_{(i,j)}(t) \tag{10}$$
$$= (1-\lambda) + p_{(i,j)}(t)(\lambda - 1) \tag{11}$$
$$= (1-\lambda)(1 - p_{(i,j)}(t)) \geq 0 \tag{12}$$

The update scheme is called pursuit-LA [7] and has rules that obey the rules of the so-called Linear Reward-Inaction (LRI) LA. The idea is to always reward the transition probabilities along with the best solution obtained so far.

4   Experiments

In this section, we present our experimental results that demonstrate the effectiveness of our approach. Although we have conducted several experiments, we will report a few representative experiments for the sake of brevity. The simulations were performed using a customized simulation environment implemented in Python.

4.1   Impact of Sensing Range and Sensor Density

The primary goal of this particular experiment is to investigate the impact of sensing range and sensor density in a vast network. At first, the experiment is performed by varying the range of the sensor between 150 m and 600 m with 70 sensors and 50 targets. Then, the next test is conducted by increasing the density of the sensors to evaluate the algorithm performance to obtain the minimum number of active sensors. Tables 1 and 2 show the obtained results of the experiment. Due to the stochastic nature of our algorithm, we report the average of an ensemble of 1000 experiments.

Table 1. Results obtained for 50 targets and 70 sensors with sensor sensing range from 150 m to 600m

Range of sensors	Average number of active sensors
150	11.752
200	8.869
250	7.557
300	7.054
350	6.694
400	6.523
450	6.512
500	6.510
550	6.465
600	6.241

Table 2. Results obtained for increasing the sensor number from 70 to 80 with 50 targets and sensing range 300m

Number of sensors	Average number of active sensors
70	2.145
71	2.140
72	2.135
73	2.120
74	2.110
75	1.967
76	1.830
77	1.549
78	1.420
79	1.347
80	1.102

From Table 1, we can observe that as we increase the sensing range of the sensors from 150 to 600 to cover the same number of 50 targets, the average number of active sensors drops from 12 to 6. Similarly, from Table 2, we can observe that as we increase the number of sensors nodes from 70 to 80 with a sensing range of 300 m to cover the same number of 50 targets, the average number of active sensors drops from 2 to 1.

Figure 3 illustrates the results from the Table 1. From the plot, we see a decline in the number of active sensors as the range increases. This is because with the increasing sensing range, the coverage area of the sensors also increases.

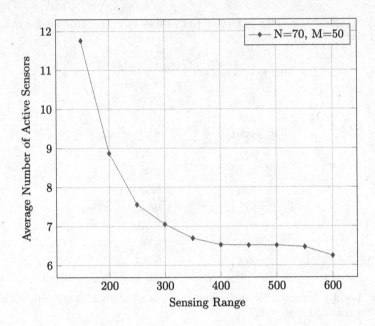

Fig. 3. A network consisting of 70 sensors and 50 targets with varying sensing range from 150 m to 600 m

4.2   Effect of the Learning Parameter

The main goal of this particular experiment is to examine the impact of the choice of the learning parameter λ on the quality of the final solution and on the convergence speed.

We vary the number of sensors between 40 and 80 while fixing the number of targets to 30. Every sensor is provided with a sensing range of 400m. The experiment is carried out by taking different values of the learning parameter lambda, "λ". Here, the value of lambda ranges from "$\lambda = 0.9$", "$\lambda = 0.99$", "$\lambda = 0.999$" to "$\lambda = 0.9999$". The results are shown in Table 3.

From Table 3, we observe that the average of the minimum number of active sensors decreases as the value of the learning parameter increases. In other terms, the quality of the obtained solution improves as the learning parameter increases. However, this comes at the cost of the convergence speed measured in terms of the number of iterations. In fact, as we increase the learning parameter, we observe the required number of iterations for reaching convergence increases too.

The results of this experiment are depicted in Fig. 4, which shows the bargraph plotting of different numbers of sensors nodes at different learning parameters. We can observe that, if the number of sensors is increased in the deployed environment, then the complexity of the problems also increases, and therefore one needs a larger value of learning parameter to achieve the optimum result.

Table 3. Results obtained with varying learning parameter lambda "λ" with sensors between 40 and 80 including 30 targets and sensing range 400 m

Number of sensors	$\lambda = 0.9$ Average number of active sensors	$\lambda = 0.99$ Average number of active sensors	$\lambda = 0.999$ Average number of sctive sensors	$\lambda = 0.9999$ Average number of active sensors
40	9.844	2.912	1.735	1.345 ☑
50	13.189	3.726	1.851	1.436 ☑
60	16.926	5.082	1.967	1.483 ☑
70	20.599	6.635	2.176	1.508 ☑
80	24.049	7.576	2.078	1.526 ☑

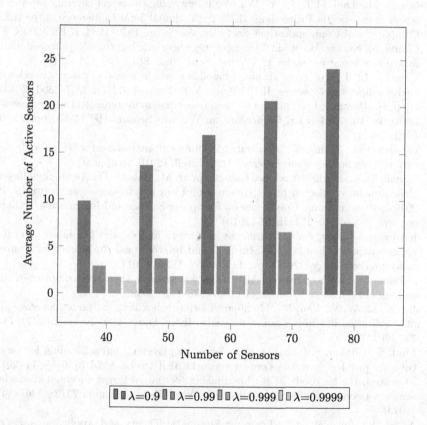

$\lambda=0.9$ $\lambda=0.99$ $\lambda=0.999$ $\lambda=0.9999$

Fig. 4. Bar plot of the data obtained in Table 3 showing the effect of increasing value of learning parameter

5   Conclusion

This paper focused on solving the target coverage problem in WSN. The sensors can select their state to be either active or sleep autonomously using the concept of pursuit LA. Comprehensive experiments were carried out to evaluate the performance of our designed algorithm. The proposed algorithm provided a methodology to find the minimum number of active sensors to cover the targets and thus addressed the issue of energy-efficient target covering in the WSN.

References

1. Agache, M., Oommen, B.J.: Generalized pursuit learning schemes: new families of continuous and discretized learning automata. IEEE Trans. Syst. Man Cybern. Part B (Cybern.) 32(6), 738–749 (2002)
2. Cardei, M., Du, D.Z.: Improving wireless sensor network lifetime through power aware organization. Wireless Netw. 11(3), 333–340 (2005)
3. Cardei, M., Thai, M.T., Li, Y., Wu, W.: Energy-efficient target coverage in wireless sensor networks. In: Proceedings IEEE 24th Annual Joint Conference of the IEEE Computer and Communications Societies, vol. 3, pp. 1976–1984. IEEE (2005)
4. Chand, S., Kumar, B., et al.: Target coverage heuristic based on learning automata in wireless sensor networks. IET Wirel. Sens. Syst. 8(3), 109–115 (2018)
5. Chen, J., Li, J., Lai, T.H.: Trapping mobile targets in wireless sensor networks: an energy-efficient perspective. IEEE Trans. Veh. Technol. 62(7), 3287–3300 (2013)
6. Diop, B., Diongue, D., Thiare, O.: Target coverage management in wireless sensor networks. In: 2014 IEEE Conference on Wireless Sensors (ICWiSE), pp. 25–30. IEEE (2014)
7. Goodwin, M., Yazidi, A.: Distributed learning automata-based scheme for classification using novel pursuit scheme. Appl. Intell. (2019, to appear)
8. Jamali, M.A., Bakhshivand, N., Easmaeilpour, M., Salami, D.: An energy-efficient algorithm for connected target coverage problem in wireless sensor networks. In: 2010 3rd International Conference on Computer Science and Information Technology, vol. 9, pp. 249–254. IEEE (2010)
9. Kittur, R., Jadhav, A.: Enhancement in network lifetime and minimization of target coverage problem in WSN. In: 2017 2nd International Conference for Convergence in Technology (I2CT), pp. 1150–1157. IEEE (2017)
10. Lakshmivarahan, S.: Learning Algorithms Theory and Applications. Springer, Heidelberg (1981). https://doi.org/10.1007/978-1-4612-5975-6
11. Lu, Z., Li, W.W., Pan, M.: Maximum lifetime scheduling for target coverage and data collection in wireless sensor networks. IEEE Trans. Veh. Technol. 64(2), 714–727 (2014)
12. Mini, S., Udgata, S.K., Sabat, S.L.: Sensor deployment and scheduling for target coverage problem in wireless sensor networks. IEEE Sens. J. 14(3), 636–644 (2013)
13. Mostafaei, H., Meybodi, M.R.: Maximizing lifetime of target coverage in wireless sensor networks using learning automata. Wirel. Pers. Commun. 71(2), 1461–1477 (2013)
14. Najim, K., Poznyak, A.S.: Learning Automata: Theory and Applications. Pergamon Press, Oxford (1994)
15. Narendra, K.S., Thathachar, M.A.L.: Learning Automata: An Introduction. Prentice-Hall, Inc., Upper Saddle River (1989)

16. Narendra, K.S., Thathachar, M.A.: Learning automata-a survey. IEEE Trans. Syst. Man Cybern. SMC **4**(4), 323–334 (1974)
17. Oommen, B.J., Lanctôt, J.K.: Discretized pursuit learning automata. IEEE Trans. Syst. Man Cybern. **20**(4), 931–938 (1990)
18. Poznyak, A.S., Najim, K.: Learning Automata and Stochastic Optimization. Springer, Berlin (1997). https://doi.org/10.1007/BFb0015102
19. Thathachar, M.A.L., Sastry, P.S.: Networks of Learning Automata: Techniques for Online Stochastic Optimization. Kluwer Academic, Boston (2003)
20. Tubaishat, M., Madria, S.: Sensor networks: an overview. IEEE Potentials **22**(2), 20–23 (2003)
21. Wu, Y., Fahmy, S., Shroff, N.B.: Optimal QoS-aware sleep/wake scheduling for time-synchronized sensor networks. In: 2006 40th Annual Conference on Information Sciences and Systems, pp. 924–930. IEEE (2006)
22. Zhang, X., Granmo, O.C., Oommen, B.J.: On incorporating the paradigms of discretization and bayesian estimation to create a new family of pursuit learning automata. Appl. Intell. **39**(4), 782–792 (2013)
23. Zou, Y., Chakrabarty, K.: A distributed coverage-and connectivity-centric technique for selecting active nodes in wireless sensor networks. IEEE Trans. Comput. **54**(8), 978–991 (2005)

Author Index

Printed in the United States
by BookMasters

Printed in the United States
By Bookmasters